This textbook is a comprehensive guide to the strategic management of information systems (IS) within businesses and public sector organisations, seeking to integrate the two, often disparate, domains of strategic management and information systems. An overriding theme is the need to manage information systems as a mixture of technical and social issues, within a broader organisational context. Corporate strategy and IS approaches are expanded and developed throughout the book, and used to synthesise a new strategic framework for information systems.

Key issues covered include:

- the essence of corporate strategy;
- IS strategy from both practical and theoretical perspectives;
- contemporary IS strategic issues;
- the technical versus social debate in IS and corporate strategy;
- ways forward for the application of strategic thinking in the IS domain;
- the integrated nature of corporate strategy and information systems as a basis for IS strategic management.

Incorporating pedagogical features such as chapter introductions and summaries, learning objectives, review and discussion questions, case exercises and a comprehensive instructor's guide, *Information Systems Strategic Management* is an ideal resource for students specialising in information systems management and those undertaking MBA programmes.

Steve Clarke is Reader in Systems and Information Management at the University of Luton. His research interests include social theory and information systems practice, strategic planning for information systems, and the impact of user involvement in information systems development.

ROUTLEDGE INFORMATION SYSTEMS TEXTBOOKS
Series Editors: Steve Clarke, Brian Lehaney *both of Luton Business School*
and D. Rajan Anketell, *Anketell Management Services*

This major new series in information systems consists of a range of texts which provide the core material required in the study of IS at under-graduate, post-graduate and post-experience levels. Authors have been chosen carefully for the scope of their knowledge and experience, providing a series designed for a range of abilities and levels. Students studying for a HND, BA, BSc, DMS, MA, MBA, or MSc in information systems, business or management will find these texts particularly useful.

1. **Security and Control in Information Systems**
   A guide for business and accounting
   Andrew Hawker

2. **Information Systems Strategic Management**
   An integrated approach
   Steve Clarke

INFORMATION SYSTEMS STRATEGIC MANAGEMENT

'Steve Clarke goes beyond the typical compendium of conventional ideas about information technology and strategic planning. His distinctive approach to the strategic management of information systems will appeal to those who wish to study information systems strategy from a critical perspective.'

Dr Frederick Wheeler, University of Bradford Management Centre

'A major strength of this book is that it does what it sets out to do, revealing that the new approach to information systems strategic management should be based upon information requirements and not upon technology. This will be an ideal text for both undergraduate and postgraduate students on courses within the disciplines of business or information systems.'

Lesley L. H. Kimber, Southampton Institute

INFORMATION SYSTEMS STRATEGIC MANAGEMENT

An integrated approach

Steve Clarke

Routledge
Taylor & Francis Group

LONDON AND NEW YORK

First published 2001
by Routledge
2 Park Square, Milton Park, Abingdon, Oxon OX14 4RN

Simultaneously published in the USA and Canada
by Routledge
270 Madison Ave, New York, NY 10016

Transferred to Digital Printing 2005

Routledge is an imprint of the Taylor & Francis Group

© 2001 Steve Clarke

Typeset in Plantin by Keystroke, Jacaranda Lodge, Wolverhampton
Printed and bound in Great Britain by
TJI Digital, Padstow, Cornwall

British Library Cataloguing in Publication Data
A catalogue record for this book is available from the British Library

Library of Congress Cataloging in Publication Data
Clarke, Steve, 1950–
    Information systems strategic management: an integrated
approach/Steve Clarke.
        p. cm. — (Routledge information systems textbooks)
    Includes index.
    1. Management information systems. 2. Strategic planning.
3. Management information systems—Case studies. 4. Strategic planning—
Case studies. I. Title. II. Series.
    HD30.213 .C55 2001
    658.4′012—dc21   00–062756

ISBN 0–415–20277–9 (hbk)
ISBN 0–415–20278–7 (pbk)

Remembering Sylvia Clarke,
as I do so often, regardless of the passing years.

Contents

Figures

Tables

Preface

THE REASONS FOR THIS BOOK

Within the many commercial organisations with which I worked during fifteen years in commercial management, strategy was, without exception, the greatest challenge to senior management. Operational and tactical issues would be attacked with relish, but strategic problems proved much less amenable to simple solutions.

During my subsequent twelve years as an academic, similar problems have been evident, both in the organisations studied and in the delivery of course material on strategy to students. Nowhere are these difficulties more evident than in attempts to apply strategic thinking to the domain of information systems. A number of reasons can be identified as contributing to these difficulties. The so-called planning/design approach to strategy, whereby, at its extreme, fixed plans are written for future strategic development, might be difficult to apply in a domain such as IS, supported as it is by rapid technological change. The human-centred nature of many IS developments may be problematic: human behaviour is difficult to predict and control, and therefore may not lend itself easily to a long-term planning approach. The focus on technological aspects of IS might be seen as diverting attention from what many regard as the real purpose of technology, which is to act as an enabler to human activity. These are just three of the many difficulties of applying strategic thinking to information systems.

In the last twenty years or so, however, strategic thinking has opened up other strategic approaches, many of which may be seen as relevant to IS, but the exploration of which appears to have been limited. The time appears right for a reassessment of information systems strategy, based on reappraisal of the two domains of corporate strategy and information systems. Within this, the primary focus is on information systems, enabled by information technology.

AIMS OF THE BOOK

The general aim of the book is to provide a theoretically and empirically grounded approach to information systems strategy (ISS). Historically, ISS has been seen as something to be 'planned' or 'designed towards' in an objective or functionalist way. This book will argue that such a view is only a limited perception of how strategy may be perceived within information systems. An alternative, presented here, is the more human-centred, participative approach to ISS. Support for this alternative view is to be found in contemporary approaches to strategy which question the design/planning school.

From this theoretical and empirical background to ISS, key issues are investigated, signposting alternative future directions. Sub-aims may be identified for each of the three parts of the book as follows.

Part 1 investigates the current empirical and theoretical background to information systems, corporate strategy and IS strategy, and how this background may be used to inform the future development of ISS. Following on from this recasting of information systems strategy, the theoretical underpinning to the domain is explored in more detail before moving on to specific issues in ISS in Part 2.

Part 2 looks at key issues in ISS, always remaining within the framework established in Part 1. These issues include: IS strategic planning; systems failure and ISS; applications portfolio and technology management; competitive advantage; the impact on ISS of organisational structure and culture; and change management.

Part 3 revisits the foundations of ISS in the light of the previous chapters, determining a strategic approach based on the theoretical and practical evidence. From this background, possible future directions are then discussed.

WHO SHOULD USE THIS BOOK?

The book is targeted at students new to information systems strategy, but with some background understanding of corporate strategy and information systems. The main audience is MBA students, but it is also aimed at supporting final year undergraduate studies in IS Management and Strategy, post-experience courses (for example, NVQ, DMS), and other Masters courses (Information Management and other courses where IM forms a key part). For MBA, this is a core subject, whilst for undergraduate, other post-experience and other Masters courses, it is more likely to be a supporting text.

STRUCTURE AND DISTINCTIVE FEATURES OF THE BOOK

The layout followed is standard for the Routledge Information Systems Textbooks series. The aim of this, together with the supplied instructors' manual, is to provide a basis for courses of academic study at the levels identified within its target audience:

- At the beginning of each of the three parts, key questions to be answered by each chapter within that part are identified.
- Each chapter begins with clear learning objectives.
- International perspectives are identified for each of the key topics.
- Case examples are provided.
- Each chapter ends with a chapter summary.
- Review questions and discussion questions are given at the end of each chapter.
- A case exercise is given for each of the main topic areas.
- Further reading is suggested at the end of each chapter.

Issues in information systems strategy are fully integrated with current thinking in corporate strategy, in particular the design or planning approach compared to the more human-centred, participative approach, which finds a parallel within IS in the growing interest in the so-called 'soft' or human-centred methods. This book aims to do justice to all strategic developments seen to be of relevance to the IS domain, ranging from the planned and political to the totally participative and emancipatory. To achieve this, key approaches to corporate strategy are addressed and related to information systems, allowing the emergence of a synthesised approach to IS strategy which is firmly grounded on current thinking.

By developing ideas from the common ground shared by corporate strategy and information systems, and incorporating within this the standard material common to most ISS texts, this book seeks to provide a more comprehensive view of strategy as it applies to IS.

USE OF THE BOOK FOR TEACHING

Each of Parts 1–3 of the book has specific objectives. Part 1 looks at the background to information systems strategy and corporate strategy, and through a critique of these determines a framework for the rest of the text. Part 2 is concerned with the core issues in ISS. Part 3 reviews the previous analysis, particularly in Part 1, and from this proposes future directions for ISS.

Consequently, depending on the aims of the course of study, students may be directed towards the different parts. In particular, for example, undergraduate study might focus on Part 2, MBA on Parts 1 and 2, and Information Management courses on the whole of the texts, with a key aim of understanding and extending the issues raised in Part 3. Where interest is mainly on practical issues, Chapter 3 can be ignored without prejudicing understanding of the rest of the text.

In terms of specific pedagogical features:

- Each chapter begins with learning objectives. Chapters are summarised, and key words and phrases listed. Questions for review and questions for discussion are given at the end of each chapter.
- References and suggested further reading, with a guide as to the relevance of the reading suggested, appear at the end of each chapter.
- Case studies and questions to be addressed by the cases are given. Generally the plan is to provide one per chapter, but some chapters may not lend themselves to the use of case material.
- A glossary is provided.

A full instructor's guide is provided on the World Wide Web:

- An instructor's manual is provided containing study guides (with lecture plans and overhead transparencies), worked examples, answers to review and discussion questions, and suggested approaches to case studies. The instructor's manual also gives suggested assignment questions not given in the main text.
- Suggested schemes of work are provided.
- The instructors' guide is split into the same chapters as the book, and for each chapter:
  - a lecture plan is given;
  - key issues are identified for the lectures, together with overhead projector slides;
  - answers to review, discussion questions and case studies are provided;
  - suggestions for assignments are given.

Acknowledgements

My first thanks go to the review panel, each member of which has offered feedback and guidance throughout the process of writing this text: their recommendations have been invaluable.

Thanks also go to all the authors and publishers who have allowed previously copyright material to be included. A book of this type relies on such support.

Finally, my thanks go to colleagues in the Luton Business School. I am sure at times they must have wondered what I was doing, but never failed to give the backup and support so essential to anyone taking on the task of producing a sole-authored text.

PERMISSIONS ACKNOWLEDGEMENTS

The author and publishers would like to thank the following publishers for permission to reproduce figures and tables:

Elsevier Science Publishers Ltd: W. Baets, 'Aligning information systems with business strategy', *Journal of Strategic Information Systems* **1** (4), 1992; N. Venkatraman, J.C. Henderson and S. Oldach, 'Continuous strategic alignment: exploiting information technology capabilities for competitive success', *European Management Journal* **11** (2), 1993 (Figure 5.1).

Gower Publishing Co. Ltd: G. Burrell and G. Morgan, *Sociological Paradigms and Organisational Analysis*, 1979 (Figure 1.1, Tables 3.1 and 3.2).

IEEE Computer Society Press: F. W. McFarlan, 'Portfolio approach to information systems', in B.W. Boehm (ed.), *Software Risk Management*, 1989 (Figure 5.8).

Jossey-Bass Ltd: C. Argyris and D. Schon, *Theory in Practice: Increasing Professional Effectiveness*, 1974 (Figure 7.2).

Management Science: B. Ives and M. Olsen, 'User involvement and MIS success: a review of research', **30** (5), 1984 (Figure 4.1).

Prentice-Hall International (UK) Ltd: C. A. Carnall, *Managing Change in Organisations*, 1990 (Figure 7.3); M. J. Earl, *Management Strategies for Information Technology*, 1989 (Table 5.1); G. Johnson and K Scholes, *Exploring Corporate Strategy*, 1993 (Figure 2.1).

John Wiley and Sons Ltd: A. D. Little, 'Technology implementation', in J. Ward and P. Griffiths (eds), *Strategic Planning for Information Systems*, 1981 (Figure 5.10); J. C. Oliga, 'Methodological foundations of systems methodologies', in R. L. Flood and M. C. Jackson (eds), *Critical Systems Thinking: Directed Readings*, 1991 (Table 3.3).

Every effort has been made to contact copyright holders for their permission to reprint material in this book. The publishers would be grateful to hear from any copyright holder who is not here acknowledged and will undertake to rectify any errors or omissions in future editions of this book.

Part 1

**STRATEGIC
MANAGEMENT
AND
INFORMATION
SYSTEMS**

CHAPTER SUMMARY

Key questions

chapter one INFORMATION SYSTEMS

- How might the domain of information systems be characterised?
- What is the impact of taking a technological view of information systems; how is this changed by a human-centred position?
- From what theoretical perspective are information systems best informed?
- How does information systems appear from a social theoretical perspective?

chapter two LESSONS FROM CORPORATE STRATEGY

- How might the domain of corporate strategy be characterised?
- Is it possible to pursue strategy as an entirely objective process?
- What different approaches are there to corporate strategy?
- Is there an integrated approach which gives a strong basis for information systems strategy development?

chapter three INFORMATION SYSTEMS STRATEGY: THE THEORETICAL FOUNDATIONS

- What social theoretical foundation is the most relevant to information systems and strategy?
- Within a chosen theoretical framework, what are the issues relevant to both information systems and corporate strategy?
- How does this theoretical underpinning apply specifically to the domain of information systems strategy?
- What does a strategic framework informed from this perspective look like?

chapter
one

INFORMATION
SYSTEMS

INTRODUCTION

In the late 1980s, the customer service department of a major electronics manufacturing and marketing organisation was looking for ways to improve communications, both among internal customer service engineers (CSEs) and with its customers. Up to that time, CSEs had relied on sales information held on a central computer, but this contained only basic sales and order data, and lacked the sort of information that customers were now beginning to expect. Examples of the questions customers were now asking on a regular basis included: future availability of product not yet manufactured; possible substitute products; the exact status of their order (not yet arrived was no longer good enough!).

Two views of how to address this surfaced within the company, which came to be known as the technology approach and the process approach: within the process approach it was recognised that an understanding of human activity was at least as important as understanding organisational or technological issues.

Those favouring a focus on technology already had a proposed solution. What was needed was a database linked to a network communications system. The database would hold all the necessary data, which could be determined according to an agreed specification. The network would enable communication between the relevant parties, using the now rapidly developing desktop computer and network technologies, in particular shared data files and electronic mail.

Protagonists of the process approach viewed this faith in the ability of technology alone to provide the answers as problematic. They did not have a solution, but rather a set of unanswered questions. How would we know when all the necessary data had been captured? Why should a computer-based communication system necessarily enable customer service engineers to work better? The list of questions became endless, and was put forward as a challenge to the over-reliance on technology as a solution to the organisation's problems. A discussion forum was arranged to determine how to progress, the outcome of which is summarised in Table 1.1.

The two sides found it difficult to reach a common understanding of the situation, and eventually it was left to senior managers to decide on the way forward. The 'technology' route offered a clear statement of the problem, a concrete solution and a means to that solution which could be monitored and controlled. The 'process' route seemed to say that 'it all depends' and, whilst offering a way forward, appeared to give no clear answers.

Perhaps unsurprisingly, the technological solution was chosen. However, with the benefit of hindsight, we can now state something else with absolute certainty: the project was abandoned without providing the anticipated benefits.

The arguments which flow from this example, which is by no means unique, are many and varied and lie at the very heart of the information systems (IS) domain. What happened was that the organisation had a problem which was a combination of human, organisational and technological factors, which it sought to solve by redefining it in purely

Table 1.1 Discussion forum outcomes

Technology	Process
The problem can be stated as the need to design a communications 'architecture'.	The problem hinges on what CSEs do, and how the organisation might better facilitate this.
The solution is a centralised database linked to a computer network.	The solution is not apparent yet. For all we know, it might not be computer-based.
The solution can be reached by approaching the problem in a step-by-step manner.	Whilst this approach is fine if you are working with technology, it does not help us when dealing with the ideas of participants in the problem.

technological terms. Why this might happen, and how such a dichotomy of views might impact the IS domain, forms the foundation for this text. Suffice it to say at the moment that the perspective taken of IS can be seen to significantly affect the approach taken and, arguably, the outcome.

LEARNING OBJECTIVES

This chapter will examine:

- the nature of the information systems domain, from theoretical and practical perspectives;

- the dominant view(s) of information systems as determined from approaches to information systems development;

- a comparison of 'hard' (technology-based) and 'soft' (human-centred) perspectives on information systems, and proposals for combining them;

- a framework for the study and practice of information systems informed from social systems theory.

INFORMATION SYSTEMS AS A DOMAIN

A study of the theory and practice of information systems soon reveals some ways in which the above example might be better understood. The demand from business organisations is for 'systems' which show an objective return in terms of cost, efficiency, effectiveness or, more typically, all three. Systems developers are driven to provide low cost solutions to perceived business problems. The management of IS becomes the design, development and management of technological solutions to identified problems. However, whilst most frequently information systems management is pursued as a predominantly technical endeavour, it none the less has to work within a given social framework.

This chapter investigates these issues further, using an area of information systems study and practical application which has been given perhaps the most attention: information systems development (ISD).

FROM TECHNOLOGY-BASED TO
HUMAN-CENTRED APPROACHES

The technology-based approach

It has been argued that the design and development of information systems (IS) has been traditionally dominated by technical, problem solving approaches, which, as can be seen from the earlier example, leads to tensions when the system to be developed is more process- or user-based. The need for discovering the requirements of users was not disputed by early information systems developers, but was typically achieved by including a user analysis stage within an existing problem solving approach. This approach, inherited from computer systems development, relied on the systems development life cycle (SDLC) as the primary method.

The systems development life cycle

Feasibility study
User requirements specification
System specification
System design
Testing
Implementation
Maintenance

The systems development life cycle is a stagewise or waterfall method, whereby each stage is undertaken in a linear sequence, generally requiring the completion of a stage before the next is commenced. So, for example, work on system design would not be authorised until the system specification was written and approved. User requirements specification fits uncomfortably into this process, since such requirements are seldom fixed but vary over the life of a project. Developers demonstrate different degrees of success in coping with this, and many become very adept at accommodating user-prompted changes.

This reflects the position reached by the early 1990s, where the waterfall model can be identified as the basis for the majority of information systems developments. A number of methodologies adhere to these principles, through which information systems development is perceived largely as a technology-based, problem solving, engineering task, approaches being geared to engineering the best solution to meet a given requirement specification within the known or anticipated constraints.

international perspective

Computer systems development at Litronix Europe

In the early 1980s, Litronix Europe, with a head office in Hitchin, England and a subsidiary north of Munich, Germany, was operating a manual order processing and invoicing system. With a turnover of some US$20 million, selling electronic components at often just a few pence each, the strain on the stock control system in particular was becoming unmanageable.

What was needed was a computerised system, but one which could handle multiple currencies and product pricing to four decimal places.

The solution was to specify a system, which, it turned out, was written as a bespoke solution. The problem could be clearly stated in terms of inputs (for example, orders, stock items), constraints (such as credit limits, stock holdings) and outputs (reports, invoices, credit lists, for example). The system to be designed was deterministic: if the inputs were known, the outputs could be predicted with certainty, given the constraints. A technological approach could be taken, and resulted in a successful working system which significantly enhanced the company's business capacity.

This was a classical functionalist solution to a standard business problem, was up and running within a year, and worked pretty well without a hitch: a prime example of the circumstances in which a 'hard' or technology-based approach is likely to prove successful.

The argument for an alternative to these technology-based approaches is supported by the findings from a number of studies of systems failure. Examples range from simple failure to meet performance goals, to catastrophic failure of the type evidenced in the London Ambulance Service and Taurus, the London Stock Exchange System. The British Computer Society has a special interest group which looks at organisational aspects of information technology (OASIG). A study by this group (OASIG, 1996) concluded that up to 90 per cent of information technology (IT) investments do not meet the performance goals set for them, and listed the technology-led nature of the process, and the lack of attention to human and organisational factors as key issues in this lack of success.

Lyytinen and Hirschheim have researched and published extensively in the IS domain. Through a thorough review of the information systems development literature (Lyytinen and Hirschheim, 1987), they make a compelling case for the argument that few information systems can be considered a success. The reason for claiming success is, they argue, largely based on an erroneous classification of how such success should be measured, which usually focuses on the extent to which the completed system meets the requirement specification laid out in advance. The main

CASE EXAMPLE

Information Systems Failure: the London Ambulance Service

The London Ambulance Service (LAS) computer-aided dispatch system failed on 26 October 1992, its first day in operation. From its inception, the system had been treated as a technical problem, to which a viable solution could be found. But LAS exhibited social and political dimensions which the technologically based approach proved ill-equipped to address.

A report on the failure (Hamlyn, 1993) makes it clear that implementation of any future system must be supported by a full process of consultation. Whilst the project management and technical aspects of the implementation were far short of that which would have been expected for this kind of project, there were in addition a number of 'human' aspects which had been inadequately considered, including poor training and incomplete 'ownership' of the system. The finding by consultants reviewing the failure that 'the computer system, itself did not fail in a technical sense . . . but . . . did what it had been designed to do' further suggested issues stretching beyond purely technical boundaries.

Following this initial failure, a new computer-aided dispatch system was successfully implemented, but only through an approach which paid heed to the whole system of concern, of which the technical system was just one interactive part.

measures are negative ones, principally the so-called correspondence failure, whereby the objectives are stated in advance, and failure is defined in terms of these objectives failing to be met. Lyytinen and Hirschheim promote the notion of expectation failure, or the failure of the system to meet the expectations of participants, as conveying a view which is more representative of all those involved in the system.

Information systems failure

Correspondence failure:	**The failure of the final 'system' to correspond with the specification determined in advance.**
Process failure:	**Failure in the development process, usually in the form of a cost overrun or inability to complete the development.**
Interaction failure:	**Users fail to use the 'system' sufficiently, effectively meaning it has failed.**
Expectation failure:	**Failure of the completed 'system' to meet the expectations of participants.**

(Source: Lyytinen and Hirschheim, 1987)

In all of these instances, the systems development life cycle emerges, implicitly or explicitly, as the prime control element, resulting in a methodology which adheres to the functional engineering model, taking a structured, problem-solving approach: human complexity in the system is seen as something which can be analysed and towards which a specification can be written. But this view is strongly challenged. Beath and Orlikowski (1994), for example, mount a convincing critique of the interaction between users and systems professionals in IS, concluding that the concentration on, and commitment to, user participation is revealed as ideological rather than actual, with users frequently shown to be passive rather than active participants in the process. They see the various systems development methodologies as containing 'incompatible assumptions about the role of users and IS personnel during systems development'.

CASE EXAMPLE

Wessex Area Health

Wessex Area Health provides health care services (hospitals, home care, doctors, health visitors and so on) within an area spanning a large part of southern England. Its computer problems are well documented. During the 1980s and early 1990s, Wessex drew up a plan to integrate the information systems provision for all of the Area Health Authority, linking hospitals, general practitioners and community health care within one system. From the beginning the project was beset by major problems.

The approach to the project was largely technological, with IBM as the main supplier of computer hardware. Computer equipment was purchased and remained unused over a year later; parts of the computer-based system that were developed failed to work as specified; care workers and doctors saw little operational benefit from the development.

Ultimately the project failed, providing little of the originally intended system, but at an estimated cost of up to £64 million (source: BBC *Panorama* documentary).

From the perspective of those involved in the development, one of the main failings was a lack of participant involvement: care staff, it is reported, referred to the computer systems developers as 'androids', because their terminology was such that they might have been from another planet. Certainly there is no doubt that the system failed; and certainly there is equally no question that it was undertaken as a predominantly technical solution to a problem that was subject to change in a highly socio-cultural environment.

If technology-based approaches cannot adequately address the problems of development for human-centred systems, what alternatives are available for this purpose?

Human-centred methods

The limitations of technological approaches to IS gave rise, in the 1960s and 1970s, to the so-called 'soft' or human-centred methods. It is argued that traditional 'engineering' approaches are 'hard' or technology-based, being premised on a view of the world which sees it as composed of determinable, rule-based systems. 'Soft' methods, by contrast, take a human-centred stance: issues are seen as determinable only from the viewpoints of human participants. Many examples are available for the use of human-centred approaches to IS, including, for example, soft systems methodology and interactive planning, which rely on a more holistic view: to understand an information system, the technology, organisation and human activity need to be addressed interdependently, not as separate, independent issues. This, it is argued, is more representative of the domain.

CASE EXAMPLE

The Barchester* Community Health information system

In 1994–7, the Barchester Health Authority undertook a complete redevelopment of its community health information systems. Community health served a trust covering over 250,000 people and employing 1200 staff. The Trust operates four hospital units and forty-five other sites, including health centres and clinics. The community information system supports teams located at each of these sites, comprising eleven multi-disciplinary community health care teams.

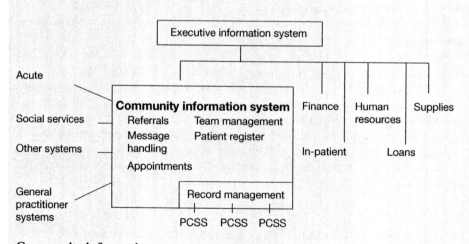

Community information system: structure and interfaces

continued . . .

The services provided are wide-ranging, and include health visiting, district nursing, community psychiatric nursing, chiropody, family planning, physiotherapy and school health. The culture of the community health care teams is a caring one, consisting mostly of community nursing and therapy staff. The views of employees are, however, highly divergent, giving rise to the problems associated with arriving at a consensus from a plurality of viewpoints. In 1994, the present community information system was eight years old, and consisted of eighty computer terminals across thirty-four sites serving twenty-one professional groups totalling over 450 staff.

The system was seen to be of limited operational benefit, having as its prime task the provision of central statistical information. The figure summarises the project to replace this system, the main purpose of which was the facilitation of more integrated patient care with greater continuity. The new computerised information system was to keep this existing system as the core, but aimed to cater more thoroughly for the needs of the operational teams, liaise with personal clinical support systems (PCSS) and, by linking to other key systems both operational and corporate, provide information to management via the executive information system (EIS). The development of this system intended to follow a piloting process, in which the pilot teams would be at the centre of the process in an essentially human-centred method.

Health care teams were invited to bid to be the pilot system, and, from the bids, two teams were chosen: one to host the pilot implementation, the other to act as a quality control group to the project. Workshops were held to share findings, check accuracy and acceptability, provide the opportunity to question and raise issues, consult on outstanding issues and to 'reassure and enthuse'.

Project outcomes

The project leader perceived the situation to be one in which a participative approach was indicated, and initially the development was pursued along these lines, aiming to determine a specification which covered the needs of users. However, following the appointment of a consultant funded by the regional head office, the intervention took a more technological direction. The main thrust moved to cost-benefit analysis, supported by activity sampling. It was concluded that a system based on personal distributed computing, using lap- or palm-top computers, would be needed.

A pragmatic, structured approach was therefore taken, focused on specifying and developing a computer-based system. Management sought a working system and, whilst accepting the need for it to meet the requirements of participants, saw this as a secondary goal. The problem became compounded, in the view of the project leader, by the consultant interpreting management pressure as a need to expedite the working system and relegating participation to a status below that of the need to determine the specification for system development. The overall solution treats the problem situation as a technical one, evidenced by considerable time spent on hardware definition, communications design, record design, functional specifications, information flows and so on. Eliciting the views of participants was handled within this technology-based,

continued . . .

structured framework. It is the view of the participants that management pressure gave rise to the system's failure to deliver the hoped-for benefits at an operational level.

Although the hoped-for participative or 'soft' approach did not succeed in this development, and as a result the hoped-for improvements in operational terms did not materialise, this and other empirical evidence from the health services sector in the United Kingdom nevertheless points to benefits to be derived from the 'soft' approach.

* Barchester is a pseudonym.

Interactive planning (Ackoff, 1981), which has been widely applied to information systems development (ISD), provides a good example of the human-centred approach. The purpose of interactive planning, in general terms, is to form a view of the system of concern through the eyes of participants, and to use this to manage the development process. A key part of interactive planning is the process of idealised design. Ackoff argues that ends are of three types: *goals* – ends that are expected to be obtained within the period covered by a plan; *objectives* – ends that are not expected to be obtained until after the period planned for, but towards which progress is expected within that period; and *ideals* – ends that are believed to be unattainable but towards which progress is believed to be possible. Interactive planning works backwards through these by: specifying ideals; determining objectives; and identifying goals. Once this is done, means can be chosen to meet the ends. So the core of the planning process lies in idealised design, which is a design of a system that: 'its designers would like to have right now, not at some future date' (Ackoff, 1981: 105).

According to Ackoff, idealised design facilitates participation, helps in generating consensus, stimulates creativity, and enlarges the designers' conception of what can be implemented. These factors, together with the requirement that the system 'designed' must specifically be capable of adapting to changes in the views of stakeholders, and the explicitly recommended use of brainstorming to specify the desired properties of the system, further situate interactive planning as a strongly human-centred methodology.

Human-centred approaches have added much to the IS domain, but the following section pursues an argument that neither technology-based nor human-centred methods offer an adequate perception of information systems: the approach must combine the best features of both approaches in relation to the given problem context.

international perspectives

The systematic versus systemic problem: systems development in the Jordanian Ministry of Tourism

Tourism is a major source of foreign revenue to Jordan, and information about past, present and potential tourists is a valuable asset. Up until the mid-1990s, the Jordanian Ministry of Tourism maintained this information on a mixture of paper-based and IT-based systems. Significant enhancements to the tourist information systems were then undertaken, based on networked IT systems. Initially the developments were primarily focused on IT, but as the development progressed this took more account of the views and activities of participants, mostly middle management, in the existing organisation. To arrive at the required system, it was not enough to form an objective view of the record systems required and computerise them; a more holistic perspective was seen to be needed, the outcome of which has been a much improved information system.

COMBINING TECHNOLOGY-BASED AND HUMAN-CENTRED APPROACHES: MIXED METHODS

The recognition of the merits of 'hard' and 'soft' approaches to IS has given rise to a number of methods of IS development which may be categorised as mixed, three of the most widely used of which have been ETHICS, multiview, and client-led design.

ETHICS (**E**ffective **T**echnical and **H**uman **I**mplementation of **C**omputer-based **S**ystems: Mumford, 1994) is a socio-technical methodology, developed in the 1970s to combine organisational, administrative and quality-of-working-life factors. Although essentially a goal-directed methodology which retains a technological system as its primary target, ETHICS none the less gives much greater concentration to the micro-social impact of ISD. It is orientated towards problem solving, working from a system requirements definition, but building into the process the views of participants. ETHICS is best suited to problem contexts where design of a system is the primary concern, but where this needs to be supported by debate within a non-coercive environment. The methodology is a problem-solving one, following the steps of defining: the mission (what ought to be, not what is); information inputs and outputs; efficiency and job satisfaction contributors; efficiency and job satisfaction reducers; and variances.

Multiview is based on the assertion that at any stage of information systems development the approach is contingent on the circumstances met at that stage. It differs from traditional systems development life cycle (SDLC) based methodologies in that it is not seen as step by step problem solving, but as an iterative process in which different approaches may be used at different times. Multiview accepts the view that no one method-ology can be seen to work in all cases, and that the methodology to be chosen cannot be decided in advance of the problem situation being known. There is explicit recognition within multiview of the need for participation.

international perspective

Mixing methods at British Gas

In the early 1990s, British Gas (BG) was undergoing considerable downsizing. BG was split into twelve regions and a headquarters, and had historically been bureaucratic, hierarchical and political, status orientated, with a blame culture. There had been little competition, with staff accustomed to high levels of job security. The impact of information technology had been low.

The effects of privatisation and increased competition forced change, with a more outward focus (towards customers, exploration and so on). The organisation was split into four companies, with the aim of reducing the status culture and generating empowerment within a non-blame culture characterised by open communications. The common systems necessary to these changes were seen to imply high informa-tion technology and information systems usage and lower core staffing levels. Staff rationalisation led to significant redeployment, and BG had set up an outplacement support function to support personnel through to redeployment within the organisa-tion or placement outside. A project to provide computer-based outplacement support was conceived as a result of the need to manage a workforce reduction of at least 25,000 plus by the year 2000. Prior to development of the computer-based system, such support was informal, using third parties as recommended by the personnel department. The system had to supply:

- curriculum vitae preparation;
- counselling;
- training;
- job search;
- information centres;
- distance learning;
- re-employment.

continued . . .

The project began with the information systems developer (ISD) setting up two exploratory sessions, using rich pictures (from soft systems methodology) and brainstorming to surface the issues. The key problems that emerged were: a need to define the specific information requirements, including the required functionality of the system; a decision regarding the number of installations and life of the system; the nature of reports required and their frequency; the external links to and from the system.

A research project was undertaken to find out what was needed. The ISD saw the problem situation as having a complexity which resulted from the human activity within the system. It was decided that two computer-based systems would be developed: one to manage the outplacement centres and one to provide management information. The actual system was developed by prototyping. Problems encountered were overcome participatively.

Project outcomes

The intervention was a mixture of technology-based and human-centred approaches, with a frequent need to cross over from one to the other. This was facilitated by an information systems developer (ISD) whose style was highly participative, reflective and self-critical. Consequently the intervention used a participative approach leading to a structured development. The problem context exhibited a complexity resulting from the high level of human activity, with the 'solution' being seen as relatively simple. The choice of brainstorming techniques in exploratory sessions showed an appreciation of the problem context, and the initial choice of participative methods was relevant. The interacting issues which emerged during the intervention were managed by the use of the methods chosen.

This proved to be a good example of mixed methods in practice, although, when the project progressed to systems development, a highly contingent, prototyping approach was taken. The evidence suggests that this resulted in the specification being fixed, with the ISD, it transpired, making ongoing amendments to the specification as the system developed, coming to decisions to satisfy participant needs which were assumed to be agreed by all.

Client-led design (CLD) was developed as a result of the argument that, since information systems result from social interaction, participants in that interaction ought to be central to systems analysis and design. CLD is therefore a genuine attempt at perceiving ISD as a primarily social process. Information systems development from this perspective needs to be *driven* by interpretivism: at the technical development stage, functionalism should not be allowed to take over. The methodology follows a five phase development:

1 appreciation of the problem situation;
2 definition and representation of the information system;
3 definition of technical support for the system;
4 implementation of proposals;
5 maintenance.

It has been argued that IS as a domain can no longer be seen as concerned primarily with the implementation of technological solutions. An information system *is* a human activity system, and as such must be studied from a human viewpoint, albeit *enabled*, where relevant, by technology.

The study of human activity is the subject matter of social theory, and it is therefore to this domain that many have turned to shed more light on IS.

INFORMATION SYSTEMS AS SOCIAL SYSTEMS

The complex nature of the systems movement means that this section can be only a cursory review of the issues relevant to ISD. A more thorough examination from a theoretical perspective is undertaken in chapter three.

Systems

The general systems movement can be traced to Bertalanffy's work on open systems theory in the 1920s and 1930s (Bertalanffy, 1950) and general system theory (GST) in the 1940s, the details of which were reproduced in full in 1968 (Bertalanffy, 1968).

This thinking has a direct application within the study of IS. A technological approach to IS reduces the complexity of the system of study, and attempts to define it in terms of rules and procedures by which given inputs can be turned into predictable outputs: a so-called deterministic system. A human-centred approach is quite different. Human activity systems are 'complex' and 'adaptive', and cannot be fully described in terms of rules and procedures. To understand better how such systems may be understood requires recourse to social theory.

Social systems

If information systems are to be seen as social systems, what kind of social system are they?

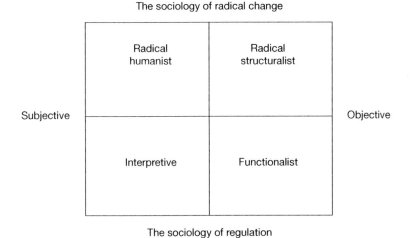

The sociology of radical change

| Radical humanist | Radical structuralist |
| Interpretive | Functionalist |

Subjective — Objective

The sociology of regulation

Figure 1.1 **Four paradigms for the analysis of social theory**

Source: Burrell and Morgan (1979: 22)

Many information systems theorists have found the Burrell and Morgan grid (Figure 1.1) to be the most applicable categorisation of social theory within the IS domain. According to Burrell and Morgan (1979), all social theories can be categorised within this four-square grid, and all social theories positioned into one of four paradigms: functionalist, interpretivist, radical humanist and radical structuralist, according to the extent to which they were subjective versus objective or regulative versus radical. These issues are dealt with more fully in chapter three, but in general this can be seen as paralleling the technology/human-centred debate in IS. A purely technological approach may be perceived as viewing the domain from a standpoint of external reality, towards which a specification can be written: an objective, unchanging specification for an unchanging reality. By contrast, a human-centred approach views reality as a product of individual consciousness: the subjective view that, without the human observer, there is no reality.

Burrell and Morgan saw the sociology of regulation as emphasising a view of society based on preservation of the status quo, whilst the sociology of radical change is 'concerned with man's emancipation from the structures which limit and stunt his potential for development' (Burrell and Morgan, 1979: 17). Again, this carries an important message for information systems as a domain, where the technology/human-centred debate may be seen as firmly lodged in the sociology of regulation, with the dominant approaches fitting within the functionalist and inter- pretivist boxes, leaving the upper half of the grid untroubled by IS developers. A more detailed discussion in chapter three develops these arguments.

CONCLUSIONS

This chapter has undertaken a critical review of the IS domain. The early view of IS, from a technological perspective, as functionalist, 'hard', problem solving is seen to be an impoverished one, over-focused on the use of computer technology. 'Soft' or human-centred methodologies have been pursued as a solution to this problem, and have been to some extent successful. But recent thinking questions the ability of 'hard' and 'soft' approaches to achieve the agenda that was apparently set out for them, and points to a need to combine approaches under the umbrella of social theory.

SUMMARY

- The nature of the information systems domain emerges, from both practical and theoretical perspectives, as consisting of 'hard' technology-based elements and 'soft' human-centred elements, in an uncomfortable co-existence. There is a perceived need to combine both 'hard' and 'soft' approaches in order to better serve the technical and social aspects of information systems.
- The dominant view of information systems appears clearly as one premised on computer systems development. As an example, human or social requirements are incorporated into the predominantly systems development life cycle process of ISD, but always remain within the constraints set by a goal-directed technical development.
- A comparison of 'hard' and 'soft' perspectives points to the value of a mixed methodology, and examples of such methodologies are given. However, even in these cases, the underpinning theoretical analysis demonstrates the problematic nature of such an undertaking and the need to combine 'hard' and 'soft' methods in a framework informed from social systems theory.
- A social framework is suggested, and an outline of its relevance to IS discussed. This issue forms the core of the argumentation of chapter three.

REVIEW QUESTIONS

1 Why might the domain of information systems be viewed as problematic? What gives rise to the basic tensions in the study of IS in general, and in the performance of ISD in particular?

2 What has been the main approach to information systems development? What alternative approaches have been pursued?

3 How would you categorise information systems failure? Why might correspondence failure be an inadequate view?

4 What is the difference between a 'hard' approach to IS and a 'soft' approach?

DISCUSSION QUESTIONS

1 Drawing on your own experience, discuss how a 'hard' or technology-based approach to ISD might be undertaken. How does such an approach allow for the perceptions of all participants (the involved and affected) in the development process? What shortcomings are to be found in this approach?

2 What do functionalism and interpretivism mean to a social theorist? Is this view helpful to information systems developers?

---

case exercise

ABC Manufacturing is undergoing a complete overhaul of its manu-facturing process. New product orders require a multi-skilled approach, which the present production-line methods are ill-equipped to provide. A decision has been taken to move to flexible teams, with each team member assigned to multiple jobs. ABC has the in-house skills to make this change, but has called you in as a consultant to look at systems to support flexible team working.

You have identified the problem to be one of providing a medium for communication and control within the factory environment, linking senior and middle management, and reporting activity at an operational level.

1 How could you undertake this task using a technology-based approach? What would be the benefits and shortcomings of such a method?

2 What additional benefits would be forthcoming with a human-centred approach?

3 How would a human-centred approach result in a developed system? If you see this to be problematic, could a mixture of the two methods be used, and if so how?

4 What has social theory to say about the theoretical issues raised by this problem?

FURTHER READING

Burrell, G. and G. Morgan (1979) *Sociological Paradigms and Organisational Analysis*, London: Heinemann.
As the source drawn on by so many information systems authors when seeking a grounding in social theory, this book is an essential reference.

Hirschheim, R. and H. K. Klein (1989) 'Four paradigms of information systems development', *Communications of the ACM* **32**(10): 1199–1216.
Although this is a journal paper, rather than a text book, the information contained is the perfect starting point for looking at information systems from a perspective of social theory.

Walsham, G. (1993) *Interpreting Information Systems in Organisations*, Chichester, Sussex: John Wiley.
Geoff Walsham has brought together in this text all the key issues in information systems from an interpretivist perspective. Although some areas are a little underdeveloped, the book is very readable, and a good starting point from which to form an alternative to the more common functionalist perspective.

Wetherbe, J. C. and N. P. Vitalari (1994) *Systems Analysis and Design: Best Practices*, St Paul, MN: West.
For those requiring a stronger grounding in information systems, predominantly from a functionalist perspective, this book is a solid source of information.

REFERENCES

'Hard' methods

System development life cycle: see, for example, Wetherbe and Vitalari, 1994.

'Soft' methods

Soft systems methodology: Checkland, 1989.
Interactive planning: Ackoff, 1981.

Mixed methods

Client-led design: Stowell, 1991.
ETHICS: Mumford, 1994.
Multiview: Wood-Harper *et al.*, 1985.

Ackoff, R. L. (1981) *Creating the Corporate Future*, New York: John Wiley.

Bansler, J. P. and K. Bodker (1993) 'A reappraisal of structured analysis: design in an organizational context', *ACM Transactions on Information Systems* **11**(2): 165–93.

Beath, C. M. and W. J. Orlikowski (1994) 'The Contradictory structure of systems development methodologies: deconstructing the IS–user relationship in information engineering', *Information Systems Research* **5**(4): 350–77.

Bertalanffy, L. v. (1950) 'The theory of open systems in physics and biology', *Science* **3**: 23–9.

Bertalanffy, L. v. (1968) *General System Theory*, New York: Braziller.

Boehm, B. W. (1989) 'A spiral model of software development and enhancement', in B. W. Boehm, *Software Risk Management*, Washington, DC: IEEE Computer Society Press pp. 26–37.

Burrell, G. and G. Morgan (1979) *Sociological Paradigms and Organisational Analysis*, London: Heinemann.

Checkland, P. and S. Holwell (1998) *Information, Systems and Information Systems*, Chichester, Sussex: John Wiley.

Checkland, P. B. (1981) 'Rethinking a systems approach', *Journal of Applied Systems Analysis* **8**(3): 3–14.

Checkland, P. B. (1989) 'Soft systems methodology', *Human Systems Management* **8**(4): 273–89.

Eden, C. (1988) 'Cognitive mapping', *European Journal of Operational Research* **36**: 1–13.

Eden, C. and P. Simpson (1989) 'SODA and cognitive mapping in practice', in J. Rosenhead (ed.), *Rational Analysis for a Problematic World*, Chichester, Sussex: John Wiley.

Flood, R. L. and W. Ulrich (1990) 'Testament to conversations on critical systems thinking between two systems practitioners', *Systems Practice* **3**(1): 7–29.

Friend, J. (1989) 'The strategic choice approach', in J. Rosenhead (ed.), *Rational Analysis for a Problematic World*, Chichester, Sussex: John Wiley.

Hamlyn, B. (1993) *Report of the Inquiry into the London Ambulance Service*, London, Prince User Group Ltd and Binder Hamlyn.

Hirschheim, R. and H. K. Klein (1989) 'Four paradigms of information systems development', *Communications of the ACM* **32**(10): 1199–1216.

Lyytinen, K. and R. Hirschheim (1987) 'Information systems failures: a survey and classification of the empirical literature', in *Oxford Surveys in Information Technology*, Oxford: Oxford University Press, vol. 4, pp. 257–309.

Mason, R. O. and I. I. Mitroff (1981) *Challenging Strategic Planning Assumptions: Theory, Cases and Techniques*, New York: John Wiley.

Morgan, G. (1986) *Images of Organisation*, Beverly Hills, CA: Sage.

Mumford, E. (1994) 'Technology, communication and freedom: is there a relationship?', *Transforming Organizations with Information Technology* **A-49**: 303–22.

OASIG (1996) 'Why do IT projects so often fail?', *OR Newsletter* **309**: 12–16.

Stowell, F. A. (1991) 'Client participation in information systems design' in *Systems Thinking in Europe* (Conference Proceedings), Huddersfield: Plenum.

Ulrich, W. (1983) *Critical Heuristics of Social Planning: A New Approach to Practical Philosophy*, Berne: Haupt.

Walsham, G. (1993) *Interpreting Information Systems in Organisations*, Chichester, Sussex: John Wiley.

Wasserman, A. I., P. A. Pircher, D. T. Shewmake and M. L. Kersten (1986) 'Developing interactive information systems with the user software engineering methodology', *IEEE Transactions on Software Engineering* **SE-12**(2): 326–45.

Wetherbe, J. C. and N. P. Vitalari (1994) *Systems Analysis and Design: Best Practices*, St Paul, MN: West.

Wood-Harper, A. T., L. Antill and D. E. Avison (1985) *Information Systems Definition: The Multiview Approach*, Oxford: Basil Blackwell.

chapter
two

LESSONS FROM
CORPORATE
STRATEGY

INTRODUCTION

In the mid-1990s, Abbott Training[1] ran an IT training organisation which spanned the United Kingdom. As the complexity of the business increased, the partners saw a need to link all of their training establishments and trainers, many of whom worked from home, to improve the integration of their training services. As network technologies were becoming more widespread, Abbott decided to commission a study into how they could build a strategy for improved integration over the medium and long term. The strategic document, when produced, abounded with 'workstations', 'hubs', 'routers' and various other technical specifications, but said little about how the network was to be used. The sole concession to usability seemed to be a statement that: 'Once the network infrastructure is in place, the organisation will be able to use it for whatever it needs.' Unfortunately, this optimism proved ill-placed, and by 1999 the network, which was installed and running at an equipment cost alone of some £5,000 per workstation, was being used almost exclusively for electronic mail.

---

1 Abbott Training is a pseudonym.

What are we to understand from this and other similar examples of IS strategy formulation and execution? Just as the domain of information systems is characterised by a debate concerning technology-based or human-centred approaches, so this problem is paralleled in information systems *strategy* (ISS). In over twenty years' involvement with dozens of organisations in the UK, Germany, Malaysia, Mauritius and the USA, I have yet to see a cohesive, integrated information systems (IS) strategic planning process. The primary reason for this can be traced in almost every case to a focus on technology. Whilst information technology strategic planning is a necessary part of any organisation's strategy, it is only part of a much wider and more complex process. The difference between information systems (IS) and information technology (IT) will be investigated further in chapter four, but its relevance here can be seen from parallels in the domain of corporate strategy, approaches to which are investigated in this chapter.

LEARNING OBJECTIVES

This chapter will examine:

- the general nature of corporate strategy;

- different perspectives through which strategy may be viewed, focusing particularly on the planning and patterning approaches;

- an integrated approach to strategy as design or discovery as a basis for information systems strategy;

- strategy applied to different organisational contexts.

CORPORATE STRATEGY: PLANS OR PATTERNS?

Strategy

Generalship, the art of war; management of an army or armies in a campaign, art of so moving or disposing troops or ships or aircraft as to impose upon the enemy the place and time and conditions for fighting preferred by oneself.

(*Concise Oxford English Dictionary*, 1974)

The definition of strategy given in the box may fit well with concepts of competitive advantage or competitive strategy. However, strategic management in business organisations is deeper and more complex than this. Whilst there is a wide variety of categorisations of corporate strategy, two extremes frequently emerge as polarised strategic views: is strategy something which can be planned, or does it just surface as the result of organisational activity for which no discernible plan is evident? Mintzberg (1987) characterises this debate as the distinction between a plan and a pattern, whilst other authors (for example, Quinn, 1980; Johnson and Scholes, 1993) refer to planned or emergent/incremental strategies.

Strategy as a plan or strategy as a pattern?

'Ask almost anyone what strategy is, and they will define it as a plan of some sort, an explicit guide to future behavior. Then ask them what strategy a competitor or a government or even they themselves have actually pursued. Chances are they will describe consistency in past behavior – a pattern in action over time. Strategy, it turns out, is one of those words that people define in one way and often use in another, without realizing the difference.'

(Mintzberg, 1987)

This distinction between strategy as a pattern and strategy as a plan is pursued throughout this book as a key issue to be resolved in IS strategic management. Is it possible, in the IS domain, to write objective strategic plans, agreed on by all concerned and forming the basis of future development? Or are IS strategies just patterns of activity which, whilst evident subsequent to their emergence, cannot be seen in any prior plans of action?

The planning approaches to strategy may be seen as developed from the so-called design school (Ansoff, 1964), which in turn can be traced to scientific reductionism. Ansoff refers to such an approach as: 'a succession of different reduction steps: a set of objectives is identified for the firm, the current with respect to the objectives is diagnosed, and the difference between these (or what we call the "gap") is determined'. Strategy is then concerned with finding those 'operators' which are best able to close the gap. What we have here is a process that is seen as objective, and as a result may be criticised for its limited attention to human activity. The design school 'places primary emphasis on the appraisals of the external and internal situations' (Mintzberg, 1990). Whilst it does consider organisational values, managerial values and social responsibility, Mintzberg's view is that these are almost always given secondary attention.

Key features of the design school

- **Complete strategy formation always precedes implementation.**
- **Responsibility for strategy rests with senior management, who are placed in a command and control position in relation to the environment.**
- **Strategy is to do with process, not content, and is a creative act.**
- **Strategies emerge from the design process, fully formulated and ready to be chosen. There is no room for an emergent view.**

An analysis of the pitfalls of strategic planning (Mintzberg, 1994) supports a categorisation under two headings: the lack of top management support, and a climate in the organisation which is not congenial to planning. These pitfalls have one feature in common: they are attributable to those people involved in strategic planning rather than the planners themselves, hence the problems associated with planning are 'seldom technical deficiencies with the planning process or the analytical approaches' (Abell and Hammond, quoted in Mintzberg, 1994); rather they are to do with the people involved or organisational issues within the business: in either case the root of the problems is 'the nature of human beings' (Ansoff, 1965).

I now want to look more comprehensively at strategy as plans and strategy as patterns, as a precursor to the formulation of an integrated approach to strategy which might be used as a foundation for IS strategic planning.

STRATEGY: THE PLANNING VIEW

At its most extreme, the planning view of strategy would have an organisation writing a future plan, for a fixed period or on a 'rolling' basis, to which it would then be expected to adhere, and against which future performance would be assessed. Johnson and Scholes (1993) provide one framework within which such an approach could be actioned (Figure 2.1).

Using this framework, the planning process begins with strategic analysis. The environment is scanned for opportunities and threats, and

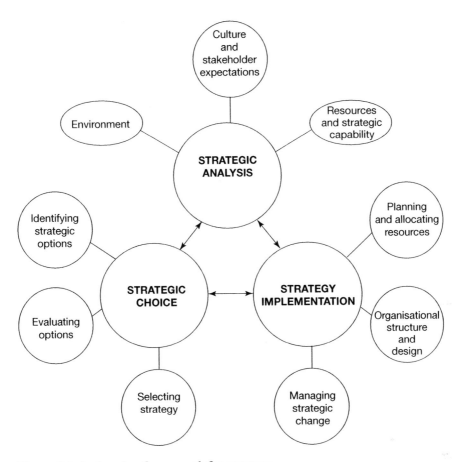

Figure 2.1 **A planning framework for strategy**

Source: Johnson and Scholes (1993: 23)

internal analysis is undertaken to determine the organisation's strategic capability, through resource and strengths and weaknesses analysis; stakeholder expectations, internal culture and power relations within the organisation are determined. Strategic choice then generates and evaluates strategic options, and selects the relevant strategies. Strategy implementation translates the chosen strategies into action, through resource planning, reviews of organisation structure and the development of systems.

This highly design orientated approach to strategic planning, whereby plans are drawn up to which the organisation is expected to work over the following planning period, is, even from a planning perspective, questionable. If such an approach were implemented, it might be expected that, for an organisation with a four-year strategic planning cycle, its activity in (say) 1998 could be found in a 1994 strategic plan. Experience, however, shows this not to be the case, and might be seen to call into question the planning process. The true position, however, is more complex, and may be seen in the way such plans are actually used: not as strict procedures to be followed or goals to be met, but as a framework within which a more flexible approach can be managed. The University of Luton, in the UK, provides an example of this. The documented strategic planning process is strongly influenced by government require-ments and results in the plan shown in the University of Luton case example.

CASE EXAMPLE

Strategic planning at the University of Luton, England

This planning framework is linked to specific goals and objectives within the planning period, and appears as a very structured, design-based approach to planning. The organisation is divided into three strategic planning domains (academic, organisational support, and resources); within each, functional areas are identified for which strategic plans are to be developed. It is common for such a framework to lead to a very structured process, with, for example, an overall mission being

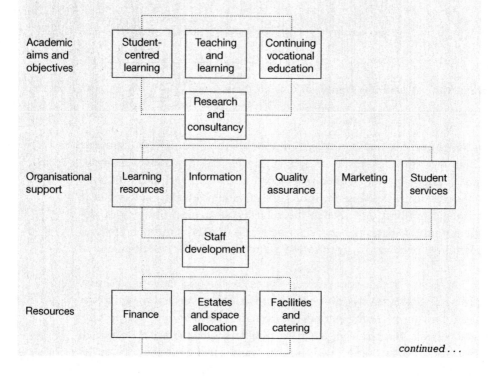

continued . . .

decided, and each functional area developing its own strategic plan in accordance with that mission.

The manner in which strategic planning is carried out in the University, however, does not strictly adhere to this, being highly participative and interactive. Strategic planning meetings, involving representatives from all parts of the organisation, are held and are used to derive the strategic aims. The needs identified within the planning framework may often be imperatives (dictated by government legislation for example), but considerable flexibility is exercised in the way in which they are achieved, and where no such imperatives exist, it is the combined view of participating groups within the organisation that is used to form the basis of strategic management.

STRATEGY AS PATTERNS OF ACTIVITY

The traditional view of strategy as a planning activity is particularly ill-suited to the domain of information systems, since it emphasises that strategy is dependent upon stability and is made unstable by change within the organisation: 'No stability means no strategy (no course to the future, no pattern from the past)' (Mintzberg, 1987). The tension between stability and change has, argues Mintzberg, led to organisations adopting two types of behaviour: one for stability and one for periods when change is required. So common is this found to be in studies of organisations that researchers at McGill University (see Mintzberg, 1987) have built a theory around it called the quantum theory of strategic change. During these periods of stability the emergent strategies continue to appear throughout the organisation but are held in check by the structure until a time arrives when the quantum leap is required.

The argument in favour of viewing strategy as patterns is that the patterns of action which we see in organisations as strategic may not have derived from any discernible plan. Citing the example of Volkswagen, Mintzberg points to the problem that, even if the organisation's plans are expressly written down, there is reason to suppose that these may not represent the true collective strategy of the organisation. Organisational theorists, agues Mintzberg, overcome this problem by the principle of attribution: 'given realisation, there must have been intention, and that is automatically attributed to the chief' (Mintzberg, 1987).

Mintzberg (ibid.) argues that 'virtually everything that has been written about strategy making depicts it as a deliberate process', whilst the evidence shows this not to be the case, with strategies emerging from the organisation without there having been a deliberate plan. Here he cites the example of the National Film Board of Canada, whose move from making *international perspective*

IBM and the quantum theory of strategic change

From its incorporation to the early 1990s, IBM achieved unrivalled and uninterrupted expansion and profits growth, based on mainframe computers from which high margins could be earned. Although small, incremental adjustments were made to meet competition from the microcomputer boom of the twenty years to the new millennium, this did not prevent IBM posting huge losses (1990–3: $14 billion; 1993: $8.1 billion), which precipitated a restructuring of the corporation.

It has been argued that one of the prime reasons for this was the intransigence of IBM senior management. Whilst sales managers, for example, commonly discussed the threat of the microcomputer boom, this message did not reach senior management, who were immovable in their belief that nothing could challenge IBM's pre-eminent position in the computer market.

That IBM has been successful in its restructuring seems not to be in question, but the corporation still stands as a prime example of the structure holding change in check until a quantum leap had to be made.

only short documentaries to a strategy based on feature films was built on the back of one film which unexpectedly ran longer than had been planned. In principle, this leads to strategy being concerned with discernible behaviour, rather than a plan as such. The pattern is a stream of realised actions which may or may not have been intended. That there may be no formal plan behind the pattern gives rise to the categorisation of strategies as deliberate or emergent; and it this emergent view that is seen in much of Quinn's work. Quinn (1980) observed that, for many organisations, whilst strategic planning forms part of the bureaucratic control process, most important strategic decisions seem to be made outside this formal planning structure. This leads Quinn to challenge the standard 'rational-analytical' approach, which he sees as normative. The goals and objectives of strategic planning are seen by him (in Mintzberg *et al.*, 1998) as determining *what* is to be achieved and *when*, but not *how* the results are to be achieved. This again is an important distinction in information systems, where the *how* of achieving the goals is contained in the programs or projects – the information technology. The rational-analytical approach is further challenged by the finding that strategic decisions, which determine the overall direction of an enterprise in the light of sometimes unpredictable internal and external change, may therefore be at the mercy of change which is not just unknown, but *unknowable*.

Since strategy may not be determinable in advance, and must deal with that which may even be unknowable, the essence is to 'build a posture' that is strong and flexible in selective ways so that the organisation can achieve its goals despite unforeseeable circumstances. The ultimate objective is to develop a position for the organisation from which it can withstand the 'unknowable' effects that are the essential components of any strategy. It is an ongoing, iterative process, arguably ill-suited to major techniques of technology development, which are problem-solving, start–end, functionalist.

A further perspective on this view of strategy can be seen from Quinn's work on logical incrementalism (Quinn, 1980; Mintzberg *et al.*, 1998). This presents an essentially collaborative view of the strategy process, within which strategy is seen as a 'fragmented, evolutionary and intuitive' process. What emerges is not a strategic plan, but a new consensus from which the organisation's way forward emerges. Logical incrementalism appears as a way to combine the planning and behavioural approaches to strategy. It is particularly strong in its ability to enable managers to respond to unforeseen change. In IS, supporting technology can be predicted in outline, but the actual technologies on which any organisation is going to pin its future are not so easy to see. The idea of logical incrementalism, whereby managers begin with a broad outline and do not commit until unforeseen issues emerge can be seen to have relevance in this context, will be followed up further in technology management in chapter five.

Logical incrementalism applied to information systems effectively takes the position that all of the events which will shape the future of a company cannot possibly be predicted, and that therefore the best that any manager can do is to look at a range of possible forces and outcomes. The objective is to decrease the risk of major failure and to increase the company's flexibility to meet the future options.

The contrast between the planning/design school and the pattern/incremental/emergent school has been chosen in this book as the key distinction on which to progress towards a better understanding of IS strategic management. However, other perspectives have been promoted which need to be placed in context before continuing. Johnson and Scholes (1993), for example, refer additionally to cultural, political and visionary views, whilst elsewhere can be found the structural view.

AN INTEGRATED VIEW OF STRATEGY

The argument so far points to the planning and design schools of strategy being categorised under the heading of 'strategy as a plan', whilst the incremental and emergent approaches seem to have more in common with

```
┌──────────────────────────────────────────────────────────┐
│                         ┌─── Planning school ───┐          │
│   Strategy as a plan   ┌┤                        ├ Reductionist │
│                         └─── Design school ────┘          │
│                                                            │
│                         ┌─── Incremental ───┐              │
│   Strategy as a pattern┌┤                    ├ Participative │
│                         └─── Emergent ─────┘              │
└──────────────────────────────────────────────────────────┘
```

Figure 2.2 **Strategy as a pattern or plan**

the patterning concept (Figure 2.2). The former may be further seen as reductionist, particularly in the case of the design school, whilst the latter appear as more participative methods. The cultural, political, visionary and structural views of strategy can now be related to the planning/ patterning approaches within an overall, integrated framework.

The visionary and structural views seem to fit best with the idea of a planning approach. A visionary leader will drive through strategies based on intuition, with often little regard for the views of others, whilst a structural approach will privilege organisational design above the needs and views of members of the organisation. Culture is about the beliefs and assumptions shared by people within the organisation, many of which are deeply rooted and unconsciously followed, and lends itself to a patterning approach to strategy. The political view is more difficult, being concerned more with power structures within the organisation, and may give rise to strongly supported plans, but may also work counter to their attainment.

Bringing these approaches together gives the position in Figure 2.3. Strategy is divided under two headings: strategy by design and strategy

```
┌──────────────────────────────────────────────────────────┐
│  Strategy by:      Design              Discovery           │
│                    (systematic)        (systemic)          │
│                                                            │
│                    Plan:               Pattern:            │
│                      Visionary           Incremental       │
│                      Structure           Cultural          │
│                                          Perspective       │
│                                                            │
│                           Political                        │
│                         Position/Ploy                      │
└──────────────────────────────────────────────────────────┘
```

Figure 2.3 **An integrated view of strategic approaches**

by discovery. Strategy by design encompasses systematic approaches, whereby plans are derived through objective, reductionist methods. Strategy by discovery, by contrast, requires a systemic (or holistic – concentrating on the whole as sub-systems in interaction rather than the parts or components in isolation) approaches, favouring participative methods covering the whole system of concern. As will become clear in chapter four, this distinction can be related directly to information systems, and will be key to framing IS strategy.

So much for the background to the different views of corporate strategy. But how, particularly in the IS planning process, can the decision be made as to which approach, or mix of approaches, is relevant to the given organisational context? To resolve this requires a classification of organisational context. Jackson (1987) refers to organisations as organisms, cultural entities, machines or coercive systems, whilst Mintzberg (1991) classifies organisations into five forms: entrepreneurial, machine, diversified, professional, and adhocracy. For two main reasons this latter classification is used for this book: first, it is comprehensive, encompassing the main organisational types found to be problematic in the IS domain; second, it is directly drawn from and related to strategic concepts.

STRATEGIC ISSUES IN DIFFERENT CONTEXTS

Entrepreneurial

The entrepreneurial form is common in startup or turnaround organisations, where direction or a sense of where the organisation must go (sometimes called 'strategic vision') dominates.

Entrepreneurial organisations typically exhibit visionary leadership, often by a single executive, and therefore typify the visionary approach to strategy. Concentration is on direction, or where the organisation should go.

Machine

Mass production is the most common example of machine organisations, which tend to be inward looking, concentrating on standardisation and formalisation and planning strategy in a very reductionist manner. Human issues are frequently given less prevalence in machine organisations, where the drive is for cost-benefits, often through standardisation or formalisation and expressed in the form of rationalisation and restructuring. One problem with this is that strategy is hard to change, and that therefore the

---

Sir Clive Sinclair and the entrepreneurial organisation

Sir Clive Sinclair's success in the 1960s and 1970s was based on technical innovation and entrepreneurial flair. Sinclair Electronics became hugely successful at manufacturing and selling digital watches and calculators, and later home computers. In neither case had a market for these products existed prior to their manufacture – the skill of the entrepreneur was to build a new market for innovative products. Strategically, the drive came from one man. Subsequently, in the mid-1980s, Sinclair Electronics decided to manufacture an electric tricycle, the C5. The subsequent multi-million pound losses are legendary, and point at once to the downside of visionary strategy.

---

organisation must in effect alter its configuration in order to change strategy, either reverting to entrepreneurial form or using an innovative form so that the necessary strategies can emerge.

---

international perspective

Strategic change at General Motors Europe

Car manufacture in European General Motors (GM) plants developed independently. Vauxhall Motors in England, for example, despite being part of GM from the mid-1920s, was still designing and building cars for the UK into the 1970s. Globalisation of the industry led to major change from the 1980s on, fundamentally driven by changes in the manufacturing process. A 'lean materials' just-in-time system now exists world-wide; manufacturing plants specialise in assembly, engine manufacture and so on.

Anyone entering these plants now would be struck by the change in employee attitudes. The rather 'mechanistic' views of the past have been replaced by a more entrepreneurial and innovative approach: the configuration has changed to enable the required strategic change.

Professional

Professional organisations, such as accountancy practices and universities, concentrate on levels of knowledge and skill, or proficiency, and therefore need to follow the patterning process, whereby strategic patterns are allowed to emerge from the combined actions of participants. Diversified organisations, often split into autonomous divisions, must concentrate strategically on the markets to be served or some other concentrated effort which brings the diversification together. The adhocratic form exhibits a drive for learning, adaptation and innovation, and may often have much in common with the professional organisation.

---

international perspective

Professional adhocracy at Swinburne University

Subsequent to gaining university status in 1993, Swinburne University Business School, in Melbourne, Australia, began to plan in earnest to improve its research activity and output. But the seeds of high-level research had already been sown. As much as ten years before becoming a university, key members of staff in the Business School were engaging in research activity, which was later to become the focus of the School's and University's strategy. The University was able to take advantage of professional, adhocratic activity, and rapidly build strategies based on it.

Diversified

In the diversified organisation, concentration on a range of products or services is paramount, often leading to autonomous business units. Strategies from the main corporation tend to focus on financial performance, whilst within each business unit the strategic thrust is towards new or improved products and services to gain a competitive edge.

Adhocracy

Here, the organisation of skilled experts, facilitated by fluid structure and informal communications, is the norm. Adhocratic organisations need continually to adapt and learn, innovating ideas for themselves and their customers.

Co-operation or competition

Added to the main forces and forms detailed above are the possibilities of forces for co-operation or competition becoming pre-eminent, leading to ideological (such as a Kibbutz) or political (for example, government bodies) forms.

It should not be expected, of course, that an organisation will adhere to any one of these forms, but rather that a mix of forms will be relevant in any given organisational context. In addition, political and ideological factors need to be taken into account within the strategic approach. Ideology is the set of beliefs and norms that bond a group of people together – a force for co-operation; whilst the political force will generate coercion and conflict – a force for competition.

CONCLUSIONS

So how may the domain of strategic planning be characterised, and what messages does this convey for strategic information systems planning?

The inescapable conclusion is that corporate strategy cannot rely on any one approach, but must craft a combination of strategic methods to fit the organisational form and context. Planning from an objective perspective is by its nature relatively short term, since it is not possible to see into the future. The purpose of such planning becomes that of formalising the process, which requires stability in order for it to work and therefore mitigates against change, which requires a flexible environment. The whole process stifles creativity. The whole essence of planning seen in these terms fits the moonshot model, whereby everything is supposed to move in predictable patterns whilst we plan our own response to it. Mintzberg's conclusion is that 'strategic planning is actually incompatible with serious strategy making' (Mintzberg, 1994); meanwhile other authors point to clear difficulties in strategic forecasting: 'Long range forecasting (two years or longer) is notoriously inaccurate' (Hogarth and Makridakis, 1981).

Mintzberg's view is that formal planning processes are useful only for undertaking and controlling the strategies which have been already formulated. The creation of strategy cannot be achieved through a formal process to craft strategy, argues Mintzberg, but requires the recognition of discontinuities which will affect the future strategic direction of the organisation, and for this the organisation must be looking at its patterns of behaviour and the patterns of others, not planning for some perceived known future based on a known past: this process had to do with 'vision and involvement . . . [not] . . . analytic technique' (Mintzberg, 1987).

Strategic management from this perspective is therefore concerned with fostering flexibility within a broad strategic framework, whilst building on emerging patterns. Planned strategy has its place but, pursued on its own, it is seen to rest on two basic misconceptions (see above right).

A clear problem emerges here in relation to information systems, since what is required in IS strategic planning is not the forecasting of some repetitive pattern or predictable event, but the 'forecasting of discontinuities',

---

The two misconceptions of planning strategy

1 That humankind stands in a predict and control relationship with the environment: 'We shall refer to the period for which the firm is able to construct forecasts with accuracy of, say, plus or minus 20 per cent as the planning horizon of the firm' (Ansoff, 1965: 44). The impact of environmental influences cannot be predicted in this way; a more realistic approach would be to see humankind as living in tune with a changing environment.

2 Senior management are detached and objective, and manage based on hard information deriving from technology-based information systems. Mintzberg (1994) sees this as 'dangerously fallacious'. Information theory has long told us that detaching information from its context strips it of its meaning, and that basing decisions on such objective, detached information runs a high risk of failure.

---

of which the technological developments which so often enable information systems are a prime example. The answer is not to attempt to forecast such discontinuities, since such forecasting is clearly impossible, but to react once they are identified. Similarly, an over-reliance on hard data may lead to an ignorance of the soft information upon which so many decisions need to be taken.

Charles Handy and strategic unpredictability

'I met a firm the other day and they said that 80 per cent of this year's turnover came from products that they had not even thought of last year . . . I don't know what the customer will want. I don't know who the customers will be. I don't know what the products of tomorrow will be. Few people can predict that.

(Handy, 1995)

In chapters one and two we have considered the general nature of information systems and of corporate strategy. In chapter three, approaches to strategy currently dominant in the information systems domain will be assessed.

SUMMARY

- Seeing corporate strategy as an objective process through the 'rational-analytical' model leads to an impoverished view of the domain. A number of alternative approaches are worthy of consideration.
- Corporate strategy is enriched by considering a number of perspectives. These include culture, structure, the visionary leader, incrementalism, politics, strategy as a plan and strategy as positioning. All these perspectives can be categorised according to the extent to which they support strategy as a rationally planned exercise or strategy as the management of emerging patterns of activity in an organisation.
- As an integrative framework for strategy, the distinction between systematic, design-focused and systemic, discovery orientated can be seen to encompass the major strategic views.
- The belief that strategy can be approached from an entirely objective position is illusory. Strategy largely consists of 'planning' for the unknown, and as such must make use of subjective judgement.

REVIEW QUESTIONS

1 Explain the different approaches to strategy as a planned sequence of actions compared to strategy as the management of patterns of activity.

2 Under the design approach to corporate strategy, are the plans generated meant to be followed to the letter? If not, what is their purpose?

3 What does an incremental/emergent approach to strategy have to offer to IS strategic planners?

4 Can any organisation afford to follow any one approach to strategic planning? According to what criteria might a synthesised approach be crafted?

DISCUSSION QUESTIONS

1 Strategy by design may be seen as well suited to a mechanistic organisation. Using as an example any organisation of this type with which you are familiar, discuss why a strategic approach based entirely on efficiency from restructuring might prove inadequate. What alternative strategic approaches could be of value in these circumstances?

2 The idea of strategic planning by managing patterns of actions is appealing, but leaves the manager with no plan to manage from. How might management resolve this problem, and what could the management process look like under this view of strategy?

3 The visionary needs a crystal ball to see into the future, but no such aid to planning exists. Is visionary strategic management ultimately doomed to failure, or does it have a place in the strategy of organisations?

---

case exercise

On page 30–1, the University of Luton strategic planning framework was outlined. The University wishes to use this framework as a basis for a participative planning exercise, aimed at determining future strategy by drawing on the knowledge and experience of those involved in and affected by the system of concern.

1 Assess the likely viability of the University's objective as stated above.
2 What problems might be encountered in using a fixed planning process as the core of a participative strategy?
3 What can be learned about this from a comparison of the design–discovery approaches to strategy?
4 Propose an approach which, in your view, offers a way forward for the University.

FURTHER READING

Ansoff, H. I. (1965) *Corporate Strategy: An Analytic Approach to Business Policy for Growth and Expansion*, New York: McGraw Hill.
Recommended as an introduction to the early work on strategy, where the design school was at the height of its influence. Still highly relevant in the more mechanistic organisational contexts.

Johnson, G. and K. Scholes (1993), *Exploring Corporate Strategy*, Hemel Hempstead, Herts.: Prentice-Hall.
Though seen by many as rather planning orientated, this is still one of the most comprehensive introductory books in the field. Johnson and Scholes actually cover most of the strategic views outlined in this chapter, but the discussion of some areas is limited, and for these Mintzberg, Quinn and Ghoshal's book should be used.

Mintzberg, H., J. B. Quinn and S. Ghoshal (1998) *The Strategy Process*, rev. European edn, Hemel Hempstead, Herts.: Prentice-Hall.
This book is a must for anyone wanting to get a basic idea of the different approaches to strategy. It is made up of contributed chapters from the key authors in corporate strategy, and covers in greater detail much of the material introduced in this chapter.

REFERENCES

Ansoff, H. I. (1964) 'A quasi-analytical approach of the business strategy problem', *Management Technology* IV: 67–77.

Ansoff, H. I. (1965) *Corporate Strategy: An Analytic Approach to Business Policy for Growth and Expansion*, New York: McGraw-Hill.

Handy, C. (1995) 'Making sense of the future', *Leadership and Organization Development Journal* 16(6): 35–40.

Hogarth, R. M. and S. Makridakis (1981) 'Forecasting and planning: an evaluation', *Management Science* XXVII: 122.

Jackson, M. C. (1987) 'Systems strategies for information management in organisations which are not machines', *International Journal of Information Management* 7: 187–95.

Johnson, G. and K. Scholes (1993) *Exploring Corporate Strategy*, Hemel Hempstead, Herts.: Prentice-Hall.

Mintzberg, H. (1987) 'Crafting strategy', *Harvard Business Review* 65(4): 66–75.

Mintzberg, H. (1990) 'The design school: reconsidering the basic premises of strategic management', *Strategic Management Journal* 11(3): 171–95.

Mintzberg, H. (1991) 'The effective organization: forces and forms', *Sloan Management Review* 32(2): 54–67.

Mintzberg, H. (1994) 'Rethinking strategic planning. Part I: Pitfalls and fallacies', *Long Range Planning* 27(3): 12–21.

Mintzberg, H., J. B. Quinn and S. Ghoshal (1998) *The Strategy Process*, rev. European edn, Hemel Hempstead, Herts.: Prentice-Hall.

Quinn, J. B. (1980) *Strategies for Change: Logical Incrementalism*, Homewood, IL: Irwin.

chapter three

INFORMATION SYSTEMS STRATEGY: THE THEORETICAL FOUNDATIONS

INTRODUCTION

Chapter one identified a need to counter the technological view of IS, through a combination of hard, technology-based and human-centred approaches, by mixing methods within a framework informed from social theory. Chapter two pointed to the planning approach to corporate strategy as only a partial view of the domain, highlighting a need for multiple perspectives within an integrative, 'discovery–design' framework embracing human-centred and technology-based positions. The indications are that information systems and corporate strategy share a common theoretical underpinning in social theory, which this chapter will investigate.

The investigation begins with a study of social theory, reviewing arguments which are cast as paradigmatic, and assessing potential future directions. To establish the theoretical underpinning, the relevant philosophical, ontological, epistemological and methodological issues are outlined and placed in context with the development of natural scientific and social theory. Social systems theory is expanded and related to IS and strategy, and a comparison is made between the problem-solving or 'structured' and alternative 'soft' approaches within these domains. Evidence is drawn from management science, providing a basis for the development of a relevant theoretical underpinning within critical social theory. Exploration of this area leads to the branch of critical social theory to be applied, and pursues this line of reasoning through critical systems thinking to a synthesised, integrated approach to information systems and corporate strategy, within a critical framework which is true to the principles of critical social theory.

LEARNING OBJECTIVES

This chapter will examine:

- an approach to social theory through which the relevant theoretical underpinning may be determined;

- information systems and corporate strategy seen in terms of a social theoretical framework;

- critical social theory as a relevant basis for information systems and corporate strategy;

- critical systems thinking as the specific theoretical underpinning to the two domains.

SOCIAL THEORY: THE PARADIGM PROBLEM

Within information systems, the categorisation of social theories undertaken by Burrell and Morgan (1979) has been used to inform the domain. This perspective views information systems as social constructs, and enables a more informed analysis of the hard–soft debate and an assessment of what may lie beyond it. Similarly, whilst not widely followed in studies of corporate strategy, the commonality of this field with IS indicates the relevance of such a social theoretical approach to strategic thinking.

Burrell and Morgan positioned all social theories into one of four paradigms: functionalist, interpretivist, radical humanist and radical structuralist, according to the extent to which they were subjective versus

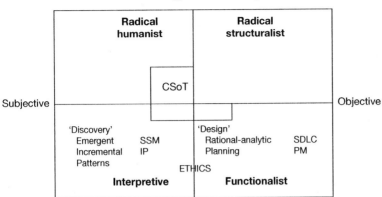

The sociology of radical change

Note: CsoT = critical social theory; IP = interactive planning; PM = project management; SDLC = Systems development life cycle; SSM = soft systems methodology.

Figure 3.1 **A categorisation of approaches to IS**

objective or regulative versus radical. Figure 3.1 shows this categorisation, together with a positioning of information systems methodologies (Clarke and Lehaney, 1999).

The aim of this classification was to show that all *social theories* could be analysed according to the extent to which they are subjective or objective and regulative or radical. The subjective/objective dimension has been discussed at length in chapters one and two, and is mirrored in the technology-based versus human-centred positions in IS, and the design versus discovery debate in strategic management. The regulation/radical change perspectives were touched upon, in so far as all IS methodologies (Figure 3.1) are cast as regulative: in other words, from the perspective of social theory, they do not have the power to change the status quo within an organisation or problem context.

It is stressed here that the positioning of methodologies is based on my subjective judgement and is open to challenge. To some extent, *where* they are placed is less important than the theories and processes which lie behind the judgements made.

Subjective versus objective

The subjective–objective dimension mirrors the hard–soft position, and can be seen in terms of four elements: an ontology, an epistemology, a view of the nature of human beings, and methodology (Table 3.1).

Table 3.1 **The subjective–objective dimension**

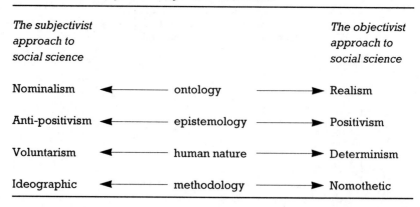

The subjectivist approach to social science			The objectivist approach to social science
Nominalism	←	ontology	→ Realism
Anti-positivism	←	epistemology	→ Positivism
Voluntarism	←	human nature	→ Determinism
Ideographic	←	methodology	→ Nomothetic

(Source: Burrell and Morgan, 1979: 3)

The ontological debate concerns the nature of reality, the two opposing extremes of thought being realism: that reality is external to the individual and is of an objective nature; and nominalism: that reality is a product of individual consciousness.

The ontological debate

The classical ontological puzzle in philosophy may be stated as: 'When a tree falls in a forest, and there is no one there, does the falling tree make a noise?' The realist would argue that noise is a property independent of human perception, and that therefore a noise would be made irrespective of whether anyone were there. The nominalist, seeing noise as a product of human perception, would disagree.

To many this argument seems rather over-theoretical, but think of it in an IS context. Suppose that you need to determine, for a part of your organisation, how to facilitate an improvement in internal communication and information sharing. You could decide that the answer is to install a computer network through which members of the department can exchange messages and information on an informal and formal basis. Of course, this is a not uncommon approach, but it is also not unusual to find the network under-utilised. Perhaps a better approach would be to see the solution to the information sharing problem in terms of the views

continued . . .

> of participants, and rather than implementing a technical solution, to investigate the situation through those views.
>
> Anyone undertaking this type of study effectively has an ontological choice: to see an objective reality in the computer equipment, or a subjective reality in the perceptions of participants.

Epistemology is concerned with the grounds of knowledge, or how the world might be understood, and this understanding communicated as knowledge. The two opposing extremes are positivism: knowledge is hard, real and capable of being transmitted in a tangible form; and anti-positivism: knowledge is soft, more subjective, based on experience and insight, and essentially of a personal nature.

> **Epistemology**
>
> Following the ontological puzzle above a little further: if asked to gather and disseminate knowledge about a computerised information systems network, the epistemological positivist and anti-positivist will behave quite differently. The positivist will study the tangible objects – the computer, its connections, software and so on. The anti-positivist will study the opinions of those using the network, and see the problem in more subjective terms. If you do not see this as a problem, try reading a typical networking plan – most are composed of technical 'mumbo jumbo' meaningless to the average user.

Human beings may be viewed on a scale from deterministic: determined by situations in the external world and conditioned by external circumstances; to voluntaristic: they have free will, and create their environment.

The view taken of ontology, epistemology and the nature of human beings directly influences the methodological approach which is adopted. A realist ontology, positivist epistemology and view of human beings as largely deterministic leaves nomothetic methodologies as the appropriate choice. Such methodologies are characterised by a search for universal laws that govern the reality that is being observed, leading to a systematic approach. From this can be derived the hard, technology-based methods in information systems and the planning/design position in corporate strategy. A nominalist ontology, anti-positivist epistemology and view of human beings as largely voluntaristic indicates ideographic methodologies as appropriate: the principle concern would be to understand the way an individual interprets the world, with a questioning of external 'reality': hence the human-centred approaches to IS and the discovery perspective in corporate strategy.

Seen in these terms, the technology-based approach to IS and the design-focused strategic methods are therefore seen as closest to the objectivist position, which, at its extreme, takes little account of the views of participants. Human-centred methods in IS, and the 'discovery' position in corporate strategy, by contrast, see 'reality' as embodied in the views and opinions of those involved in and affected by the system of concern.

Regulation versus radical change

The regulation–radical change dimension (Table 3.2) was the result of Burrell and Morgan recasting the then prevalent order–conflict debate. The sociology of regulation emphasises a view of society based on preservation of the status quo, whilst the sociology of radical change is 'concerned with man's emancipation from the structures which limit and stunt his potential for development' (Burrell and Morgan, 1979: 17).

The functionalist paradigm is, in Burrell and Morgan's terms, regulative in nature, highly pragmatic, often problem orientated, and applying natural scientific methods to the study of human affairs (ibid.: 26). The early application of functionalism to business organisations is to be found in functionalist organisation theory, which can be traced from

Table 3.2 **The regulation–radical change dimension**

The sociology of regulation is concerned with:	*The sociology of radical change is concerned with:*
The status quo	Radical change
Social order	Structural conflict
Consensus	Modes of domination
Social integration and cohesion	Contradiction
Solidarity	Emancipation
Need satisfaction	Deprivation
Actuality	Potentiality

(Source: Burrell and Morgan, 1979: 18)

the work of F. W.Taylor (1856–1915). This laid the foundation for the 'classical school', contributors to which have been, for example, Fayol and Gulick. In Fayol's work, organisations are characterised in terms of a reality which can be investigated systematically, taking a highly mechanistic view of human beings, informed by an objectivist ontology and epistemology.

Functionalist organisation theory can be identified anywhere from the most objective to the most subjective margin of the paradigm. The relevance of this to IS is that the incorporation of, for example, user requirements analysis into structured methods could be seen as simply moving the method towards the interpretive end of the functionalist paradigm. Consequently, the functionalist or technology-based approach to IS does not preclude the incorporation of user or participant views, but it does determine that they are taken from a *functionalist* position. The parallel in corporate strategy can be seen in attempts to include participant involvement within a planning framework, where it must be recognised that the participation is constrained within the limits of that framework – the 'plan'. With this approach, the existing structure becomes the main focus of attention: the 'real world' which exists independently of human perception. As social theory suggests, such an approach serves to support the existing power base.

As with the functionalist paradigm, the interpretive paradigm is also regulative, seeing social reality as 'little more than a network of assumptions and intersubjectively shared meanings' (Burrell and Morgan, 1979: 29–31). Burrell and Morgan argue that the ontological assumptions of interpretive sociologists lead them to seek an understanding of the existing social world from an ordered viewpoint, and do not allow them to deal with issues of conflict or coercion. Interpretivism suffers criticism from all sides. Functionalists see it as finding out about problem situations without any means of solving problems or, in effect, producing any 'hard' output. Radical thinkers criticise interpretivism for its support of the status quo – the existing power base: interpretivism is fine for achieving consensus, provided the conditions required for consensus-seeking pre-exist; it has no means of overthrowing existing power structures or of resisting coercion.

Human-centred approaches to organisational problem contexts adhere to the interpretive paradigm. Mostly working through debate, these methodologies work well in a forum where debate is not constrained, but are unable to secure these conditions where they are not already to be found. In corporate strategy, for example, the organisational context may be one in which the need to collect the views of all involved in the system of concern has been identified (as might be the case in a professional organisation such as a university). However, the debating forum established for this may contain coercive influences (for example, managers who suppress certain viewpoints), or may be composed of members whose abilities in contributing to debate are unequal. Soft methods provide few remedies for these situations.

The 'hard' and 'soft' of strategy formulation in UK higher education

Higher education institutions in the United Kingdom are required to prepare and submit strategic plans, in a prescribed format, to the Funding Council for Higher Education. But the planning process is highly bureaucratic, and may be seen as having little to do with the management of such institutions.

　　The solution adopted by many is to undertake strategic management as a participative exercise, using the outputs to help in the preparation of the required plans.

　　However, the two forms of strategic management, one very structured and the other highly interpretivistic, sit uncomfortably together, and arguably would be better replaced by a more cohesive, integrated approach able to embrace both perspectives.

The radical humanist paradigm has much in common with the interpretive paradigm, but unlike interpretivism has a radical intent, emphasising 'the importance of overthrowing or transcending the limitations of existing social arrangements' (Burrell and Morgan, 1979: 32). The emphasis is on radical change and the attainment of potentiality through human emancipation, or release from 'false consciousness': 'the consciousness of man is dominated by the ideological superstructures with which he interacts, and these drive a cognitive wedge between himself and his true consciousness. This . . . "false consciousness" inhibits or prevents true human fulfilment' (ibid.).

The radical humanist paradigm was highlighted in chapter one, in the form of critical theory, as a worthwhile direction promoted by Hirschheim and Klein (1989). Hirschheim and Klein view functionalism as the 'orthodox approach to systems development', seeing it as means- and ends-dominated but with little discussion about the ends, since these are taken as given: 'there is one reality that is measurable and essentially the same for everyone . . . the role of the developer is to design systems that model this reality'. But the ends can seldom be assumed to be agreed, and in modelling reality the question of whose reality becomes paramount. Whilst Hirschheim and Klein see an alternative in interpretivism, in so far as it does not accept there to be an objective reality but only socially constructed reality, their view is that its relativist stance makes it '*completely uncritical* of the potential dysfunctional side effects of using particular tools and techniques for information systems development'. Different systems development outcomes are simply viewed as the result of different socially constructed realities. The radical humanist paradigm offers a way forward. Through critical social theory there is the possibility of moving beyond a debate located firmly in the sociology of regulation to a critically reflective, radical position. In organisational studies, the work of Habermas (1971) has been taken to provide the primary theoretical support to underpin approaches based on radical humanism. This work is discussed in more depth below, in the section on 'Critical social theory'.

The radical structuralist paradigm shows similarities with functionalist theory, but advocates radical change through structural conflict (Burrell and Morgan, 1979: 34), which finds its place in organisation studies through forms of direct political action. Whilst a tenable view for organisational theorists, its value to the study of IS and corporate strategy is limited, since the aim is not revolution but gradual change, albeit with a radical intent.

SOCIAL SYSTEMS THEORY, INFORMATION SYSTEMS AND STRATEGY

The limitations of functionalism are demonstrated in the study of social systems, where predictive models may be seen to have only limited value. Social action does not readily lend itself to study by reductionist methods, but is determined by the meaning that individuals attribute to their actions. But the hard (technology-based) and soft (interpretivist or human-centred) methods are both cast in the sociology of regulation, and radical approaches have been demonstrated as offering a way forward from this regulative, uncritical position. This is the direction which has been pursued by part of the systems movement, from its origins in the so-called Singer/Churchman/Ackoff school (Jackson, 1982; Britton and McCallion, 1994), through to present-day systems thinkers. Jackson has shown how the soft methods of Ackoff, Checkland and Churchman all adhere to some degree to the assumptions of the interpretive paradigm, and identifies a third position which distinguishes hard, soft and emancipatory systems thinking (Jackson and Keys, 1984; Jackson, 1985). The argument is for a complementarist approach, which sees the strengths and weaknesses in each of the three areas and argues that each one must be respected for those strengths and weaknesses.

All of this is mirrored in IS and corporate strategy, where the argument is wrongly cast within the sociology of regulation. The effect of this is illustrated, in Figure 3.1, by positioning the approaches to IS and corporate strategy on the Burrell and Morgan grid. From the perspective of social theory, current approaches to information systems and corporate strategy may be classified as functionalist or interpretivist. Design approaches to corporate strategy and technology-based approaches to information systems may be seen as functionalist; discovery methods in corporate strategy and human-centred approaches to information systems interpretivist. Critical social theory therefore offers the potential for combining these approaches with a radical intent. Much work in this area has already been undertaken in the management science domain, and it is this work that is used in the following section to formulate an alternative framework for IS strategy.

CRITICAL SOCIAL THEORY

Critical social theory (CSoT) can be traced from the work of Kant (1724–1804). The two most widely accepted modern theorists are Foucault and Habermas, and it is to the latter that management science turned in the 1980s in order to develop a more human-centred view of its domain.

CSoT applied to IS and corporate strategy is appealing for its denial of the natural scientific principles on which study has largely been based hitherto. Seen through a scientific framework, IS appears as the design of a system to satisfy a known set of requirements – objective, verifiable requirements which are the same for all involved since they are independent of human opinion. Similarly, corporate strategy is seen as framing plans to be achieved in the future. CSoT refutes this, seeing our understanding of the world as determined by *a priori* conditions which are uncritically accepted. Critical theory seeks to expose these, and thereby release human beings from their 'false consciousness' to a position from which true potentiality can be attained. An alternative to these dominant approaches to IS and corporate strategy may be found in development based on the work of Habermas, in particular his theory of knowledge constitutive interests (Habermas, 1971) (Table 3.3).

Habermas sees all human endeavour as undertaken in fulfilment of three knowledge constitutive or cognitive interests: technical; practical (in satisfaction of human interaction or communication), and emancipatory. These three cognitive interests are identified in labour, interaction and

Table 3.3 **The theory of knowledge constitutive interests**

Knowledge constitutive interest	Basis of human interest	Type of interaction	Underlying paradigm	Methodological approach
Technical (control)	Labour (instrumental action)	Man–Nature	Functionalist	Empiricism
Practical (understanding)	Communicative (interaction)	Man–Man	Interpretive	Hermeneutics
Emancipatory (freedom)	Authority (power)	Man–Self	Radical/critical	Critique

(Source: Oliga, 1991)

power, and provide conditions for the three sciences, empirical/analytic, hermeneutic and critical. The empirical/analytic, served by the natural sciences, is therefore seen as satisfying only the technical interest. Since technology-based approaches to IS and the design school in corporate strategy have their roots in the natural sciences, they appear from a Habermasian perspective as an insufficient theoretical basis. What is needed in addition is social science, to service the practical (hermeneutic) interest in achieving communication and consensus, together with critical science to deal with issues of power and domination, serving the emancipatory interest.

Jackson (1993) follows the cognitive categories of Habermas, and argues that in Western industrialised society the technical interest has been accorded too much primacy. Jackson goes further in asserting, again after Habermas, that, in fact, practical questions are redefined as technical ones, effectively blocking the separation of what we ought to do from questions of how we ought to be doing it.

From these roots came the development, in the domain of management science, of critical systems thinking, which is detailed below before moving on to the development of a critical framework for IS strategy.

CRITICAL SYSTEMS THINKING

Critical systems thinking (CST) accepts the contribution of both hard and soft approaches, and, through critique, enhances awareness of the circumstances in which such approaches can be properly employed.

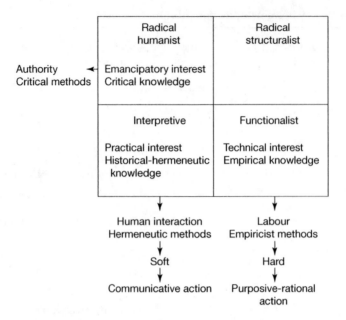

Figure 3.2 **The social validity of hard, soft and critical approaches**

The pragmatism of the hard approaches and the lack of theoretical reflection in the soft allow CST to expose both as special cases with limited domains of application. Figure 3.2 summarises this position through an expansion of the Burrell and Morgan grid (Clarke, 2000: after Oliga, 1991).

This perspective further supports the view that traditional approaches to IS and strategy largely emerge as serving the technical interest, with labour applied as purposive-rational action to achieve transformation by application of the means of production – information technology and functionalist planning methods. The alternative, evident in these domains since the 1970s but still limited in acceptance, is the service of the practical interest from the interpretive paradigm, relying on the communication of perceptions and consensus forming.

That critical systems thinking is true to the principles of critical social theory can be seen from its five key commitments (Jackson, 1991), which may be condensed to three: critical awareness; complementarism at the levels of methodology and theory; and human emancipation.

The commitments of critical systems thinking

Critical awareness '[consists of] examining and re-examining taken-for-granted assumptions, together with the conditions which gave rise to them' (Midgley, 1995). Within a strategic intervention this helps to inform the choice and mix of methodologies in relation to the changing nature of the problem contexts. Social awareness calls for the need to understand the organisational climate determining the popularity of particular systems approaches, and for full consideration to be given to the organisational consequences of the use of different methodologies.

Complementarism at the level of methodology rests on the encouragement of diversity and the concept that methodologies can do no more than 'legitimately contribute in areas of specific context' (Flood, 1990: 28), whilst complementarism at the level of theory is supported by Habermas's knowledge constitutive interests, this commitment being more usually framed as 'theoretical commensurability'. In IS, my own experience of working with computer systems developers confirms that communication across paradigms is problematic – the same words often have a different meaning to each of the groups, as is demonstrated in the case example, which is taken from an actual study.

CASE EXAMPLE

The Project: A System to Collect and Disseminate Information On Hospital Out-Patients Requiring Home Visits

The following transcript of a conversation is taken from a meeting between the systems analyst (SA) given the task of developing the above system and a group of health visitors (HV) who make use of the information and have the responsibility for reporting back to management.

SA: We need to identify user requirements for this system.

HV: Yes, without a clear picture of what the user needs, we cannot move forward.

SA: My first priority, then, is to gather together this information. I need about a month, and will get back to you all with my findings.

continued . . .

	SA perception	HV perception
User Requirement	Programmer specifications of files, records and fields	Information to support activity whilst travelling to patients
Procedure for gathering information	Observe activity of health visitors and discuss with management	By engaging with health visitors, determine what is, should be, and could be done to support their activity
Information presented	Management reports	Ongoing and report-based information from which health visiting activity can be managed and reported

These differing perceptions proved to be the major barrier to be overcome in specifying and developing the system. Had they not been addressed, the SA perception would have led to a system useful to management but of little benefit to others participating in its use.

The objective of human emancipation, from an organisational standpoint, is to enable the achievement of human potentiality, which, it is argued, is enhanced where information systems are implemented in a way that promotes human well-being.

A critical framework for information systems strategy

A theoretically and practically informed framework for ISS must therefore embrace a number of issues. First, any investigation must be conducted with hard, soft and critical intent. The latter involves examination and re-examination of assumptions and material conditions (the conditions according to which those assumptions have been made) within an emancipatory framework. The investigation must be sensitive to the given organisational climate and will demand a diversity of methods. All of this should take place within a cycle of action and learning, in which all involved and affected are included. A diagrammatic representation of such a framework is given in Figure 3.3.

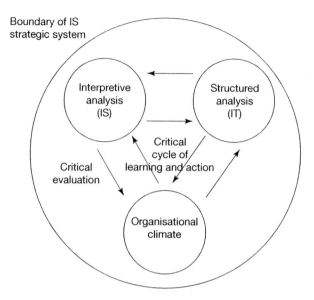

Figure 3.3 A critical framework for information systems strategy

Source: Clarke *et al.* (1999)

   The first consideration in using this critical framework is the need to set a boundary for any investigation. Since the strategic system is to be seen in social terms, this boundary should consider primarily those involved in and affected by the system. The core of the strategic study is then seen in terms of the 'critical cycle of learning and action', whereby a mix of interpretive and structured analysis may take place within the determined boundary, having regard to the given organisational context. My own view is that we should not be prescriptive about the approach taken to this, but recent research points to a number of possible approaches. First, forms of action research, in particular co-operative inquiry (Reason and Heron, 1995), offer an action learning cycle which has open participation as a primary aim. The initial objective is to investigate the system creatively through interpretive analysis with a critical intent. Methods available specifically to facilitate this task include brainstorming, lateral thinking, the use of metaphor, Ackoff's idealised design and Checkland's soft systems methodology stages one to five.

   At any stage of an intervention, it is necessary to select methods for that or subsequent stages. The work of Jackson and Keys (1984) proved a major turning point in the development of an approach to this within a critical framework. By looking at the range of problem contexts and at the systems methodologies available for addressing these contexts, Jackson and Keys provided a unified approach which draws on the strengths of

CASE EXAMPLE

The Use of Metaphor at the University of Luton in the United Kingdom

The University of Luton is a major provider of higher education (HE), with over 14,000 students. The undergraduate provision is managed through a modular credit scheme, making it similar to HE institutions in the USA and Australia.

In an investigation of information systems strategy at the University, it was proving difficult to form a strategic view of student information systems, and a decision was taken to set up brainstorming sessions with all key participant groups, using metaphor as the main investigatory technique.

Although, as facilitator, I had in mind the five key metaphors (see Morgan, 1986) of machine, organic, neuro-cybernetic, socio-cultural and socio-political, these were not used explicitly, since it was felt that the unfamiliarity of the terminology to most participants would hinder the intervention.

Participants were invited to form two self-selected groups, each nominating its own chair and note-taker, with me acting as a facilitator and explicitly not taking on the role of expert. The central issue was stated as: 'How can monitoring and recording of students at faculty level be better facilitated by information systems?' The only additional guidance I gave was in the form of questions to elicit how participants viewed the problem situation. In particular, participants were encouraged to consider, in terms of the past, present and future of the organisation, whether student monitoring and recording would be best perceived as a repetitive process which could be mechanised to improve efficiency, a collaborative 'social' process, or a process subject to determination by those in positions of power (corresponding to mechanistic, socio-cultural and socio-political metaphors).

The major problem identified by the participant groups was that of moving from a stable, bureaucratic past to a changeable and uncertain future, and participants felt it important that the impact of this on information systems development should not be underestimated. Prior to gaining University status, the University was structured to meet the needs of bureaucratic control from the local authority, with systems designed centrally to that end. The view of a changeable future initially left the institution with a mix of seemingly unmanageable demands: with centralised, inflexible systems needing to adapt to the change and being ill equipped to do so.

the relevant methodologies, rather than debating which method is best, and argues for a reconciliation focusing on which method to use in which context, controlled by a 'system of systems methodologies' (SOSM). A number of developments have followed this initial work, from which Midgley (1995) summarises the key approaches that may be seen as having adequate theoretical underpinning and practical potential as: total systems intervention (TSI) combined with SOSM; the creative design of methods; critical appreciation, and TSI reconstituted (see box).

Choice of methods using total systems intervention

In the most recent version of TSI, the system of systems methodologies has been replaced by the 'complementarist framework' (Flood, 1995: 183) in which the five metaphors are aligned with processes of design (technology-based methods), debate (human-centred methods) and disimprisonment (critical methods).

Designing	*Debating*	*Disimprisoning*
Machine	Socio-cultural	Socio-political
Organic		
Neuro-cybernetic		

In this framework, type of method can be chosen by asking which of the following questions is most pertinent: how should we do it: this is addressing issues of design, and must therefore assume that consensus already exists; what should we do: addressing issues of debate, and therefore assuming non-coercive consensus is achievable; who will benefit/why should we do it: addressing issues of disimprisoning, where disagreement, power or coercion are prime.

CONCLUSIONS

Functionalist science, on which much of IS and corporate strategy has hitherto been based, can no longer be defended as objective, value free, theory neutral, but is to be seen as maintaining and strengthening existing power relations. Interpretive science recognises 'reality' as socially constructed, but is unable to overcome *a priori* conditions and false consciousness and is therefore conservative in orientation. Critical science has the potential to overcome these limitations.

An analysis of sociological paradigms exposes both technology-based and human-centred approaches to information systems strategy (ISS) as regulative, and as an insufficient basis for the domain. IS strategic management needs to be viewed from a radical humanist position if it is to progress. Habermas's critical social theory, and specifically his theory of knowledge constitutive (technical, practical and emancipatory) interests, which can be thought of as spanning the functionalist, interpretivist and radical humanist paradigms, offers a way forward from this position. Habermas's critical social theory provides the philosophical underpinning to critical systems thinking (CST), which in turn is of value in strategic management, where a combination of functional, interpretive and critical issues must be considered.

From the theoretical argument of this chapter, a critical framework for ISS has been developed (Figure 3.3), which will be used as a point of reflection for the strategic issues in the ensuing chapters.

SUMMARY

- The analysis based on the sociological paradigms of Burrell and Morgan has provided a categorisation of approaches to ISS which has enabled critical development.
- ISS seen from this perspective is best positioned within the radical humanist paradigm.
- Within this paradigm, a relevant theoretical underpinning to IS and corporate strategy is to be found in the critical social theory of Jurgen Habermas. Developments in critical systems thinking, based on Habermasian theory, are seen to be particularly relevant to ISS.
- A framework for IS strategic management based on this has been developed, and is presented within this chapter.

REVIEW QUESTIONS

1 What are the paradigmatic issues involved in relating social theory to the domain of information systems strategy?

2 Explain the currently dominant positions in information systems and strategy. What are the limitations of these positions in theoretical terms?

3 What is Habermas's theory of knowledge constitutive interests? What does this tell us about human social activity?

4 What are the 'commitments' of critical systems thinking? How may these be seen as underpinned by the knowledge constitutive interests of Habermas, and what guidance do they offer for information systems strategy?

DISCUSSION QUESTIONS

1 The subjective–objective dimension in social theory may be seen as fundamental to an understanding of how theory underpins information systems strategy. Discuss the components of the subjective and objective positions, and explain, with practical examples, how strategy might be approached from each of these perspectives.

2 With the help of examples, discuss why conventional approaches to information systems and corporate strategy might be regarded as regulatory. Why is this a problem, and how might the problem be resolved?

3 Discuss the proposition that the critical theory of Habermas and critical systems thinking form a clear theoretical basis from which to build a critical framework for information systems strategy. What is the nature of this framework, and how could it be used in an actual strategic intervention?

---

case exercise

The Alpha Marketing Agency employs fifty consultants, all of whom have equal responsibility for securing new business and servicing the client base. Whilst all are multi-skilled in marketing terms, each individual has particular talents which are called upon as required by others. The method of working is through informally constituted, flexible groups which come together for a particular task or set of tasks and are then dissolved. The groups work in an open-plan office with no allocated desk space and with access to mini conference rooms as required.

For some time there has been a concern that the future of the Agency is unpredictable, and hence uncertain, and the consultants all agree that some form of strategic planning is necessary.

How would you approach the strategic planning and strategic management of this organisation? What theoretical issues do you see as relevant to this particular organisational context?

FURTHER READING

Burrell, G. and G. Morgan (1979) *Sociological Paradigms and Organisational Analysis*, London: Heinemann.
An essential text for understanding the components and application of social theory. Very readable, and applicable to business organisations.

Flood, R. L. and M. C. Jackson (eds) (1991) *Critical Systems Thinking: Directed Readings*, Chichester, Sussex: John Wiley.
A collection of papers from key authors in the area of critical systems thinking, which will give anyone new to the subject a good grounding.

McCarthy, T. (1978) *The Critical Theory of Jurgen Habermas*, London: Hutchinson.

Held, D. (1980) *Introduction to Critical Theory: Horkheimer to Habermas*, London: Hutchinson.

Roderick, R. (1986) *Habermas and the Foundation of Critical Theory*, Basingstoke, Hants.: Macmillan.

Habermas's writings on critical theory make difficult reading, and for those wanting a guide to the area these three texts are more accessible.

Ulrich, W. (1983) *Critical Heuristics of Social Planning: A New Approach to Practical Philosophy*, Berne: Haupt.

Ulrich's text is often cited as a source for his methodology, critical systems heuristics, which is aimed at interpretive situations distorted by coercion. Its main strength in my view, however, lies in its exposition of Kant's critical theory. Generally an excellent text for anyone wishing to explore further this theoretical area.

REFERENCES

Britton, G. A. and H. McCallion (1994) 'An overview of the Singer/ Churchman/Ackoff school of thought', *Systems Practice* 7(5): 487–522.

Burrell, G. and G. Morgan (1979) *Sociological Paradigms and Organisational Analysis*, London: Heinemann.

Clarke, S. A. (2000) 'From socio-technical to critical complementarist: a new direction for information systems development', in E. Coakes, R. Lloyd-Jones and D. Willis (eds), *The New SocioTech – Graffiti on the Long Wall*, London: Springer Verlag (2000).

Clarke, S. A. and B. Lehaney (1999) *Human-centred Methods in Information Systems Development: Is There a Better Way Forward? Managing Information Technology Resources in Organisations in the Next Millennium*, Hershey, PA: Idea Group Publishing.

Clarke, S. A., B. Lehaney and Y. Nie (1999) 'Critical theory as a foundation for strategic management', in *Synergy Matters: Working with Systems in the 21st Century* (conference proceedings), Lincoln School of Management, Lincoln: Kluwer Academic and Plenum.

Flood, R. L. (1990) *Liberating Systems Theory*, New York: Plenum.

Flood, R. L. (1995) 'Total systems intervention (TSI): a reconstitution', *Journal of the Operational Research Society* 46: 174–91.

Habermas, J. (1971) *Knowledge and Human Interests*, Boston, MA: Beacon Press.

Hirschheim, R. and H. K. Klein (1989) 'Four paradigms of information systems development', *Communications of the ACM* 32(10): 1199–1216.

Jackson, M. C. (1982) 'The nature of soft systems thinking: the work of Churchman, Ackoff and Checkland', *Applied Systems Analysis* **9**: 17–28.

Jackson, M. C. (1985) 'Social systems theory and practice: the need for a critical approach', *International Journal of General Systems* **10**: 135–51.

Jackson, M. C. (1991) 'Five commitments of critical systems thinking', in *Systems Thinking in Europe* (Conference Proceedings), Huddersfield: Plenum.

Jackson, M. C. (1993) 'Social theory and operational research practice', *Journal of the Operational Research Society* **44**(6): 563–77.

Jackson, M. C. and P. Keys (1984) 'Towards a system of systems methodologies', *Journal of the Operational Research Society* **35**(6): 473–86.

Midgley, G. (1995a) 'Mixing methods: developing systemic intervention', Hull University Research Memorandum no. 9.

Midgley, G. (1995b) 'What is this thing called critical systems thinking?', in K. Ellis, A. Gregory, B. R. Mears-Young and G. Ragsdell (eds), *Critical Issues in Systems Theory and Practice*, New York: Plenum, pp. 61–71.

Morgan, G. (1986) *Images of Organisation*, Beverly Hills, CA: Sage.

Oliga, J. C. (1991) 'Methodological foundations of systems methodologies', in R. L. Flood and M. C. Jackson (eds), *Critical Systems Thinking: Directed Readings*, Chichester, Sussex: John Wiley, pp. 159–84.

Reason, P. and J. Heron (1995) 'Co-operative inquiry', in J. A. Smith, R. Harre and L. V. Langenhove (eds), *Rethinking Methods in Psychology*, London: Sage.

Part 2

KEY ISSUES IN THE STRATEGIC MANAGEMENT OF INFORMATION SYSTEMS

CHAPTER SUMMARY

Key questions

chapter four INFORMATION SYSTEMS STRATEGY AND SYSTEM FAILURE

> - How can information systems failure be classified in order to aid understanding?
> - What is the role of user involvement in the success of information systems?
> - What approaches to involving users are available?
> - How, in summary, should IS failure be addressed?

chapter five STRATEGIC ALIGNMENT

> - How might it be ensured that information strategies and corporate strategies are aligned?
> - Once information strategies are determined, what is the process for determining the IS and IT strategies necessary to support them?
> - How might IS and IT be included in the overall strategic planning of an organisation?
> - What does this tell us about frameworks for strategic alignment?

chapter six COMPETITIVE ADVANTAGE FROM INFORMATION SYSTEMS

> - How does Porter's work underpin the study of competitive advantage?
> - Where does sustainable competitive advantage come from, and can it be generated by IT alone?
> - What makes competitive advantage sustainable?
> - Can competitive advantage be planned for, or is the best hope that we might have frameworks by which it may be understood?

chapter seven STRUCTURE, CULTURE AND CHANGE MANAGEMENT IN INFORMATION SYSTEMS

> - How can organisational structure and culture be classified?
> - Is change management best viewed from structural or cultural perspectives?
> - How is strategic change approached in the IS domain?
> - What are the relevant frameworks for change management in information systems?

chapter
four

INFORMATION
SYSTEMS
STRATEGY AND
SYSTEM
FAILURE

INTRODUCTION

No discussion of information systems strategy would be complete without considering information systems failure. Often the failure of a system is considered an operational problem: for example, a failure of definition or design. However, in recent years, as the complexity of information systems has grown and with human issues growing in importance compared to purely technical ones, it has been increasingly recognised that, both operationally and strategically, an organisation needs to encourage participation to lessen the risk of systems failure.

Information systems failure is not susceptible to a simple definition, but this chapter seeks to classify it, and relate the derived failure classifications to organisational type: in principle, the evidence suggests that organisational types or 'forms' tell us much about the kind of IS failure from which they will be most at risk.

The user involvement literature is also assessed; from this further support is forthcoming for systems failure to be viewed as a human-centred issue. Based on these findings, a proposal for involving users is proposed, in which it is argued that 'soft' methods (echoing the findings of chapters one and two) and action research offer a way forward.

LEARNING OBJECTIVES

This chapter will examine:

- a classification of information systems failure, related to organisational forms;

- the relationship between information systems success and user involvement;

- involving users: the value of action research;

- different models of action research;

- the application of action research to information systems.

TOWARD A CLASSIFICATION OF INFORMATION SYSTEMS FAILURE

Ask anyone whether they have witnessed failure of an information system and typically there will be a variety of responses, indicating different perceptions of the meaning of 'failure'. Examples may be quoted of systems failing to meet a predetermined specification; failing to be completed at all, or to be completed on time; completed but remaining unused; and so on.

CASE EXAMPLE

The Unused Office Automation System

The directors of a major manufacturing organisation in the South of England were concerned by the time lags in their administrative systems. Memos were taking several days to reach their destination, and sometimes weeks to elicit replies. The purchase order requisition and ordering system was grinding to a halt, with items ordered for production now causing major hold-ups within the manufacturing process. Something had to be done. The IT manager spoke of an off-the-shelf solution to this that would reduce paperwork and speed up the whole process. The new

continued . . .

product, costing £50,000 in computer equipment and £20,000 in application software, was ordered and installed.

Now, two years after this initiative, the purchasing department uses the computers to track its orders and invoices, but the rest of the hoped-for benefits have not materialised: other intended participants within the company simply do not use the system, preferring to continue relying on mostly paper-based communications.

There are many reasons *why* this may be so. The key issue here, however, is that the system is considered to have failed not because it will not do what was intended, or that the specification was wrong, or that it could not be delivered. The system is installed and working – but most of the time it remains unused.

In effect respondents see failure in a number of different ways, and when asked whether a system has failed respond according to their own percep-. tions. But all these examples of failure are in some way valid, and need some classificatory framework in order that the concept of IS failure may be more clearly understood. The first major attempt at such a framework was undertaken in a study by Lyytinen and Hirschheim (1987) and this is used as the basis of the classification within this chapter.

Since the concept of failure is one which is interpreted differently by different individuals or groups, the notion of system failure can be seen as a pluralistic (subject to many different views) or human-centred issue. This is important, since it refers back to the 'hard–soft' debate under-pinning Part 1 of this text. In turn, it has led Lyytinen and Hirschheim to see systems failure as grounded in social theory: systems do not fail primarily because of technical shortcomings, but because those involved in and affected by the system are not adequately considered.

Involved and affected participants in any system will have a set of expectations, and it has been suggested that the purpose of specifying a system is to capture these expectations in a form which facilitates its design and development. This is true whether the specification under consideration is of user requirements (covering user needs that the system aims to satisfy) or of the system design (usually a more technical document, including input screens and report and file specifications). Unfortunately, any written specification can only include a sub-set of the expectations of participants: this has to be so, if only because at any given time all participants will not have verbalised all of their expectations, either because they have not yet thought of them, or perhaps because they do not yet even know about them. This immediately leads to problems if systems design is defined in terms of meeting a specification, since by definition no specification can contain all of the necessary requirements: what is actually needed is for system design to meet the as yet incomplete expectations of potential users. All this is particularly relevant in organi-sational learning as we enter the new millennium, where participants' expectations increase and become refined as a system is developed and used.

This has led Lyytinen and Hirschheim (1987) to classify information systems failure into four categories: correspondence failure; process failure; interaction failure; and expectation failure. Correspondence failure is the failure of an information system to meet requirements stated in advance, and may be seen as a rational view of system development. Here it is assumed that a specification can be determined which is the same for all those who will use the system; and whilst there are undoubtedly cases where this is valid, there are at least an equal number of instances in which such a specification is unattainable. It is often argued that this is the most common form of failure, but one which leaves a number of unanswered questions, such as: what happens if the specification is wrong in the first place? does a working system that works according to specification necessarily have any value if it does not achieve what is required? and so on.

The second category of failure, process failure, occurs when a system cannot be produced within given budget or time constraints.

CASE EXAMPLE

Process Failure in The English Tourist Network Automation Project

The English Tourist Network Automation Project (ETNA) aimed to computerise the network of over 500 English Tourist Information Centres (TIC). It commenced in 1990 with the objective of providing a networked information and reservation system to all TICs within two years.

By 1993 the project had been effectively shelved, to be replaced by local, stand-alone systems. The reasons, argues Mutch (1996), have their roots in the nature of the English tourist information network, which is essentially a collection of locally administered offices, under local authority control, working loosely to a set of procedures determined by a central government agency: 'In some authorities, a corporate strategy is pursued [which] can conflict with . . . systems like ETNA.'

Abandonment of the project can be traced to a number of factors. Changes in funding within the sponsoring body did not help, but ultimately the principal reasons for failure rested on largely human issues. Mutch refers to information systems

continued . . .

as 'complex social systems': in this case the 'social' problems emerged as lack of commitment from the TICs and a resulting low prioritisation for the project. A strategic issue was also identified, in that the development was of strategic importance for the central body, but proved difficult to relate to the diverse strategies of local government.

The computing literature and the practice of computer systems development arguably focus quite strongly on this view, within which failure represents the inability on the part of the organisation to adequately manage, for example, the software development process. Perhaps the best analogy of this type of failure is found in civil engineering, where most large projects (the Channel Tunnel, Sydney Opera House, the Humber Bridge), though ultimately completed, keep to neither time nor cost estimates. In information systems development, such problems can give rise to partial completion or, in extreme cases, the complete abandonment of the project. Interestingly, from a major study of project abandonment (Ewusimensah and Przasnyski, 1991), the conclusion is drawn that the main causes 'are rooted in organisational, behavioural/political issues'.

Interaction failure represents a form of proxy measurement for information systems failure, which at its most simple assumes a system to be a success if that system is subjected to large amounts of user interaction, or, conversely, a failure if it is not used or is underused by its intended target population. Problems of this approach include, for example, the difficulty of measuring the quality of the interaction taking place, generally studied under the heading of user satisfaction. If user interaction is to be measured, should we be measuring, for example, user time on the systems or the amount of data transferred? In any event, these measures may have little to do with task performance.

Expectation failure, the failure of the information system to meet the expectations of the users, is seen by Lyytinen and Hirschheim as a superset of process, correspondence and interaction failure. As with the ETNA case, although classifiable as process failure, the underlying reasons for its abandonment are traceable to strategic and participative issues. Consequently expectation failure can be used as an overall means of assessing IS failure, within which any or all of the other failure notions may have some relevance.

These four concepts of systems failure can now be related to the organisational forms (Mintzberg, 1991: see chapter two). Table 4.1 represents a summary of empirical evidence from consultancy interventions in corporate strategy, where it has been observed that certain forms of organisation appear to make the organisation more susceptible to a particular type of *international perspectives*

Expectation failure and the problem of multiple perspectives

Interact* manufacturing management had reached the mid-1990s without using communications technologies, but felt that the time was right, in 1997, to build a local network of personal computers (PCs) to enable improved internal communications and links to the wider world of the internet.

The computer systems manager joined forces with a chosen supplier, and throughout 1997–8 achieved the implementation of a PC-based computer network linking together all management and administrative staff. The key facilities provided were electronic mail (email) and connection to the internet.

Only when the system was operational did the real problems begin to emerge. Almost daily, unsatisfiable requests were arriving. One senior manager wanted a diary facility between himself and key staff, but was told the system had 'insufficient memory'. A designer had a frequent need to send plans to a US partner: previously this had been done by mail or fax, but now he decided to email them as attachments – the US partner was unable to read them. To add to these problems, the system's disk capacity, designed for five years' use, was overflowing within three months.

This highlights the problem with the correspondence concept, in that it relies on it being possible to reach an agreed specification for a system. In this case, not only was such a specification elusive, but the flexibility required of the final system was the one thing that the specification concept proved least able to provide.

* Interact is a pseudonym.

Table 4.1 **Organisational forms and systems failure**

Organisational form	Correspondence failure	Process failure	Interaction failure	Expectation failure
Machine	**	*		
Entrepreneurial		*	*	*
Professional			**	**
Adhocratic			**	**
Diversified		**		*

system failure. The table indicates the relevance of systems failure concepts to the different forms of organisation in Mintzberg's (1991) classification: a double asterix indicates a stronger relevance.

Mechanistic organisations seem most prone to correspondence failure. In such organisations it is expected that the rule-based, machine-like processes can be specified, and systems developed towards that specification, and concentration therefore tends to be on the extent to which the finished system matches the specification laid out in advance. System failure typically appears as a full or partial failure to meet the predetermined specification.

Diversified organisations seem to suffer most from process failure. This has much to do with the traditional approach to information system development, whereby technical experts have a strong involvement in the specification and design of the system, commonly concentrating on a standard offering which can be used across the diversified structure. Problems most often occur during implementation, preventing the process being effectively completed.

Professional and adhocratic organisations are most likely to suffer interaction failure. The autonomy accorded to individuals in these types of organisations is such that any system with which they have not had ongoing involvement will largely be ignored, unless *by chance* it proves to be of value.

Interaction success and failure in an English university

In the early 1990s, senior management at the university approved the development of a centralised system for recording research performance. The system was developed, and academic staff were requested to update it with ongoing research. Academics appeared to see little value in the system, and it soon ceased to be used as the definitive record of research in the university. It has since been replaced by ad hoc local systems.

Contrast this with the same university's experiences with email. Senior management decided to provide email connectivity to all staff at around the same time as the research initiative. The perceived overwhelming need identified by management was not matched initially by the enthusiasm of proposed users, an example being resistance from users of Apple Mac computers to a system which was to be PC-based. Now the project is up and running, and is used by almost everyone in the university. It may not provide all of the functionality needed, but its benefits far outweigh these shortcomings.

Expectation failure is an important concept in any organisation where success depends on human interaction. Arguably, the only possible organisational form where this could be ignored is the machine organisation. Certainly, in professional and adhocratic organisations, if the expectations of organisational members are not taken into account, evidence suggests that ultimately the system will fail.

CASE EXAMPLE

The London Ambulance Service

The London Ambulance Service (LAS) despatch system receives calls for ambulance attendance, despatches ambulances according to resource availability, and monitors the progress of all despatched ambulances, within the Greater London metropolitan area.

This area covers around seven million people in an area of over 600 square miles. The ambulance despatch system deals with up to 2,500 calls per day. A new computer-aided despatch system was implemented on 26 October 1992, and was a project without precedent either in terms of technology or functionality. By 4 November of the same year it had been abandoned. Reasons cited for the failure of this system cover every aspect of systems failure. The main examples include:

- The CAD system was over-ambitious, untested, overloaded and had been developed and implemented against an impossible timetable. In addition the project management was poor.
- Staff distrusted the system and expected it to fail, and staff training was incomplete.
- There was a lack of consultation with users and clients in the development process: in particular, ambulance crews effectively did not participate. In addition, there was an attempt to change working practices through the implementation of the computer system.

The information that on 26 and 27 October 1992 the system did not fail in a technical sense seems to point to correspondence and process failure not being at the heart of the problem, although they were evident in the subsequent abandonment of the system on 4 November. In fact, LAS is a classic case of a system which, for a variety of reasons, failed to meet the expectations of its users.

(Sources: Charette, 1995; Robinson, 1996; Hamlyn, 1993)

Overwhelmingly, therefore, the evidence points to participation, through which all involved in and affected by the system of concern can be part of IS strategic and operational development, as the fundamental issue affecting system success or failure. In systems development, there has been considerable concentration on these issues within studies of user involvement. Additionally, the last quarter of the twentieth century has seen extensive development of participative approaches to organisations in the domain generically termed 'action research'. In the rest of this chapter, user involvement and action research are investigated as strategies to reduce system failure.

USER INVOLVEMENT AND INFORMATION SYSTEMS SUCCESS

User involvement research focuses on two outcome variables: system quality and system acceptance; but underlying these are the more complex issues of cognitive and motivational factors which *give rise to* improved quality or improved acceptance. This research is supported by the strong practical belief, drawing on empirical evidence from qualitative studies (Hirschheim and Klein, 1989; Lawrence and Lowe, 1993), that user participation is essential to the success of systems.

Lin and Hsieh (1990), drawing on ten years' work with MIS practitioners, put forward the view that 'most of these practitioners agree that in determining the success of the development project, user attitude towards system development is an important factor'. Such an attitude can be seen in a willingness or otherwise to participate in development and implementation, and the factors that may cause the users to avoid participation need to be reviewed. These factors include: senior management behaviour, from full support to unwillingness to spend; complaints about cost; corporate culture and organisational politics; and user background and personality.

Two major factors are said to affect the success of participation. First, who should be involved in the development: views vary from affected parties to top level management. The second factor to be considered is the development conditions, in particular what type of system is being developed. For highly technical systems or where systems are clearly defined and have set goals or objectives, system quality may not be improved by user involvement: 'User participation is advocated when acceptance is critical, or when information required to design the system can only be obtained from users' (Ives and Olsen, 1984).

The other important factor to consider in the development process is that user involvement may not be relevant at all stages. It may be important to choose the stage at which involvement is applied (for example, design, implementation and so on). Also the types of participation need to be carefully chosen. Types are proposed by Mumford and Henshall (1978):

Consultative: where consultation with relevant user groups is practised.

Representative: where all levels of the user group are represented in the design team.

Consensus: where an attempt is made to involve all workers in the user department through communication and consultation.

This can be taken further by looking at the degree of involvement of users, ranging from no involvement, through involvement by advice, to involvement by doing, where users are members of the design team, to involvement by strong control, where users pay directly for development from their own budgets.

Ives and Olsen (1984) suggest a model of user involvement (Figure 4.1) which illustrates the relevant issues. The success of an information system is assessed according to its perceived quality or the level of system acceptance. The factors that are seen to contribute to this originate from 'user characteristics' (primarily seen by Ives and Olsen as the roles of participants) and the 'organisational climate' (relating to the structure and culture of an organisation). Given these 'input characteristics', the type and

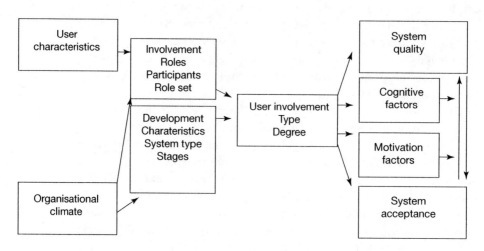

Figure 4.1 **A descriptive model of user involvement**

Source: Ives and Olsen (1984)

degree of user involvement may then be assessed according to the type and stage of system development. Cognitive and motivational factors complete the model, and may be seen as pointing to limitations or constraints placed on the achievement of system success. This model further builds on the earlier discussion of organisational forms, which gives additional richness to the 'organisational climate' issues.

User involvement and the Ives and Olsen model
Consider the case of a requirement to implement an administrative and document control system in a legal practice. The organisational form might be seen as professional, with a tension between the bureaucratic approach of administrators and the looser, adhocratic views of professional lawyers.

This tension must be dealt with through user involvement. In essence, both administrators and lawyers have a contribution to make, but will see issues quite differently. Perhaps the solution is to separate the groups, or perhaps some way can be found to combine them. Whatever the decision, a framework for type and degree of involvement will be the key to the success of this system.

Finally, in general, cognitive factors will be immensely valuable here, with highly trained and capable personnel. However, this will be constrained, particularly on the part of the lawyers, by a low motivation, seen as an unwillingness to be very deeply involved.

Whilst user involvement theory and practice is valuable for determining the nature and purpose of involvement, it says little about how it should be undertaken. Within information systems, the means of achieving user involvement has concentrated on the use of human-centred methods.

---

international perspectives

Soft methods in the formulation of information systems strategy at Richards Bay Mining

Richards Bay Mining (RB) is a mineral extraction and processing plant operated by Rio Tinto Zinc (RTZ) in South Africa. The objective at Richards Bay was to use information technology to reduce the sustainable cost of producing saleable

continued . . .

products through process control, providing better aids for decision-making, and through the use of data processing to automate clerical procedures and provide management information.

The aim of the Richards Bay project was therefore to test commercially whether a participative approach could be used in the development of an information systems strategy.

RB employs 2,600 people, forty-one of whom are engaged in information systems and fifty-two in process control systems. In 1984 a business systems planning exercise had been conducted, using an approach developed by IBM which involves a detailed mapping of business processes. The exercise was not held in high regard at RB, and management were looking for a fresh approach. Perceived problems included a lack of appreciation of the potential of information systems within the business and the difficulties of moving from the current centralised mainframe to a more flexible, integrated approach.

The approach taken at RB involved four groups of participants: a steering committee, a task force, an advisory group and a project team. The participative methods used included a mixture of recognised human-centred methods, together with Porter's industry and value chain analysis for the initial understanding of the inner and outer context. The process at RB was further enriched by the 'six thinking hats' of De Bono.

Initial workshops were designed to catch the imagination of and involve the participants, and to identify the business imperatives using Porter's five forces and value chain models, combined with PEST (political, economic, social, technical) analysis as discursive devices. The output of this phase was an agreed description of the business context, a business model with defined objectives for each part of the business, and agreed terms of reference for the task force.

The case provided an interesting example of how the tension between a participative project and use of prescribed methodologies to achieve a desired outcome was resolved. The general view of those involved in the project was that the participative approach effectively engaged a large number of people in strategy development, and demanded that those involved, and particularly managers, enquire, listen, reflect, analyse and then present their views.

Overall this approach would seem to reduce greatly the risk of a failed IS strategy development project. It ensures the strategy embodies the understanding of the management and obtains the commitment of those involved to the final outcome.

(Source: Ormerod, 1996)

Chapter one outlined the difference between human-centred and technology-based approaches to information systems; increasingly, however, in the ten years leading to the new millennium, the use of human-centred methods in information systems focused on the domain of action research (see, for example, Clarke and Lehaney, 1997; Checkland and Holwell, 1998).

ACTION RESEARCH: INVOLVING USERS IN THE STRATEGIC AND OPERATIONAL PROCESS

Within the general domain of action research, the approach which has been identified, from theoretical and empirical studies, as most relevant to information systems (Clarke and Lehaney, 1997) is human inquiry. Human inquiry relies on those involved in and affected by the inquiry expressing their views and opinions, and two primary approaches to human inquiry have been determined as valuable within information systems: co-operative inquiry and participatory action research.

Co-operative inquiry

Co-operative inquiry (Reason, 1994) is an iterative cycle of action and reflection in which is also embedded a critical process. This parallels the critical approach recommended in chapter three, and aims to expose privileged and expert positions. The relevance of this to information systems, particularly in reducing the risk of failure, should not be under-estimated. Except in situations where a technology-based system is the goal, it has been argued that participation will substantially enhance the chances of success: co-operative inquiry is a critical, participative process which is well suited to supporting human-centred interventions.

Co-operative inquiry can be operationalised through a four-phase methodology (Reason, 1994: 326). In phase 1, co-researchers agree an area for inquiry and identify research propositions; phase 2 initiates agreed actions and records outcomes; phase 3 is where participants become fully immersed in the process, and is seen to give rise to new insights; finally, phase 4 involves returning to consider the original research propositions.

Co-operative inquiry in information systems development

The co-operative inquiry process provides a quite different view of IS development compared to traditional approaches, and is of particular value where the information system is one for which a fixed specification (the standard 'hard' or 'structured' method) or even a consensus view (the usual target of a 'soft'

continued . . .

method) is unattainable. An example of such a system might be a computer-based network, the purpose of which is to improve communications and decision-making in an organisation: the structured approach works only if the requirement is turned into a technical specification; the soft approach demands a consensus or agreement which might not be forthcoming.

In such circumstances, co-operative inquiry may proceed as follows:

1 Determine a representative group of those involved in and affected by the system.
2 Identify the areas for discussion related to the system of concern, and determine key issues. This should be done participatively.
3 Undertake a programme of participative sessions. For example, it might be useful to hold an initial brainstorming session to seek new perspectives, followed by more structured approaches using relevant inquiry methods (metaphor (Morgan, 1986) and the idealised design stage of interactive planning (Ackoff, 1981) are useful here).
4 Reconvene to consider critically the results of the analysis and determine possible ways forward.

Participatory action research

The underlying theme of participatory action research (PAR: Foote Whyte, 1996) is liberation. Reason (1994: 334), however, refers to how PAR projects are dependent on people with the skill to initiate and run them, and how this, in Colombian projects, has led to outsiders being prone to 'see what should be done' possibly 'without full participation'. So there is a need to identify whose reality is to be served. Is the reality of those affected recognised, in which case they must fully participate, or is the power base being served, in which case this dominant reality is imposed on others? This is again an issue in IS, where it is not uncommon to observe an expert (usually in information technology) taking over an IS project and effectively superimposing his or her reality on the participants, often with the full support of a minority power base in the form of management.

Many of the declared features of PAR show strong similarities with information systems, including its commitment to both social and technical issues, the deployment of a variety of techniques, the promotion of organisational learning through the inclusion of participants in all elements of a study, cautioning against the use of experts, and relying on the facilitator becoming part of the community, leading to joint learning by the researchers and researched: 'The researcher must be accepted as . . . someone who comes from the outside, who wishes to do an important and useful study, but who . . . will eventually go away again' (de Olivera and de Olivera, 1982).

So in PAR an approach can be identified which is not prescriptive as to method, but which should be seen more as a generalised form of inquiry where issues such as communication, liberation and empowerment are prime. Information collected has to be organised and offered back to the group for appraisal. The aim is to produce a perceived reality and an actual reality, between which a gap will exist. The work of de Olivera and de Olivera focuses on how to identify, understand and use this gap, basing any action on the needs of participants. They see liberation within the group processes as a fundamental issue, and seek to bring this to the fore so that it may be confronted by the group. Properly conducted, such confrontation will have the effect, not of imposing a substitute reality from without, but rather of mobilising the group to develop an awareness of their own reality from within: 'the fundamental movement of militant observation consists in seizing the potential for change from the inside of each given situation and activating that potential towards what *can be*' (de Olivera and de Olivera, 1982, italics in the original).

Human inquiry offers a range of approaches to participative analysis which have been tested in the IS domain (Clarke and Lehaney, 1997) and have been shown to add considerable value to user involvement methods. Whilst in my own research and practice I have found co-operative inquiry to be the most directly relevant, there is clearly scope for a variety of human inquiry methods, drawing on all aspects of the domain.

CONCLUSIONS

This chapter began with a consideration of information systems failure, how it might be classified, and what this means in terms of the key determinants of and possible corrective measures to address such failure. Expectation failure (the failure of a completed system to meet the expectations of users) is presented as a view which may be seen as embracing all other failure types, and therefore as a sound basis on which to ground an assessment of the success of systems.

Systems failure, however, must be seen in context: empirical evidence shows that certain types of failure are more prevalent in certain types of organisation. So, for example, correspondence failure (the failure of an information system to correspond to the specification laid out in advance) is most likely to be dominant where an organisation's processes are highly mechanistic, or rule-based.

User involvement studies then point to poor user involvement as a primary cause of the success or failure of information systems, and suggestions as to how this might be addressed are drawn from the user involvement domain. Again, context proves important here: who should be involved and at what stage are dependent to some extent on the nature of the system under development. But user involvement has little to say specifically about how the involvement should be undertaken, and evidence here is sought from empirical studies which point to human-centred methods and action research as potential directions.

From all of this, IS failure emerges as a problem with both operational and strategic implications, but one which is predominantly human-centred. Examples of human-centred methods and action research being embedded into IS practice are presented, and it is recommended that this development should continue.

SUMMARY

- Information systems failure has been classified, and the failure types of correspondence failure, process failure, interaction failure and expectation failure identified. Each failure type is related to the organisational forms of machine, entrepreneurial, professional, adhocratic and diversified. Expectation failure is promoted as the most all-encompassing failure notion.
- The user involvement literature has been assessed and, as a result, success or failure of information systems is seen to depend heavily on the extent to which participants in an IS strategic development are included at a variety of stages of the process.
- A proposal for involving users has been put forward. Here it is argued that 'soft' methods, whilst substantially advancing understanding of human issues in information systems development, are to be seen as explicitly underpinned by action research. Two relevant approaches to action research are outlined, and future development based on these is recommended.

REVIEW QUESTIONS

1 Outline the different classifications of system failure, and explain the meaning of each.

2 What are the stages of user involvement for information systems

developments? What is the relevance of the degree of technical content in a development to user involvement?

3 Outline some examples of soft methods which are used in IS. How do these relate to the domain of action research?

DISCUSSION QUESTIONS

1 Expectation failure may be seen as embracing all types of IS failure. If this is to be argued, is there any value in assessing failure from alternative perspectives?

2 'Who is to be involved in an IS development is dependent on the organisational context and the nature of the problem situation.' Critically evaluate this statement.

3 It has been argued that the key to involving users in IS development rests on gaining an understanding of a soft methodology, such as soft systems methodology, and applying it in every case. Ormerod's work, and the arguments drawn from the domain of action research, seem to deny this. What is your view?

---

case exercise

Welland* Health Authority uses computers for its centralised recording and reporting functions, but these play no part in its operational management. However, the strategy of Welland calls for all community workers (health visitors, general practitioners, midwives, psychiatric care workers and so on) to function as 'composite teams'. In principle, this requires everyone working in the community to share information and support each other in pursuance of a 'holistic' care structure.

Devise a strategic and operational approach to achieve the development of an information system to better facilitate the sharing of information within a 'holistic' care structure.

* Welland is a pseudonym.

FURTHER READING

Ives, B. and M. Olsen (1984) 'User involvement and MIS success: a review of research', *Management Science* **30**(5): 586–603.
This paper summarises the literature and research to 1984, covering almost 700 published documents. Whilst the domain has moved on since 1984, this is an excellent starting point for anyone undertaking a review of user involvement. Any student would be advised to begin here, and undertake a citation index search of this paper to determine the future direction.

Lyytinen, K. and R. Hirschheim (1987) *Information Systems Failures: A Survey and Classification of the Empirical Literature*, Oxford Surveys in Information Technology, no. 4, Oxford: Oxford University Press, pp. 257–309.
Similar to the above paper, this very detailed analysis of systems failure is a seminal paper on the subject. Here is to be found the source of the classification of expectation failure and so on.

Mintzberg, H. (1991) 'The effective organization: forces and forms', *Sloan Management Review* **32**(2): 54–67.
Though extensively published elsewhere, this is the original source of Mintzberg's classification of organisational forms used in this chapter.

Reason, P. (1994) 'Three approaches to participative inquiry', in N. K. Denzin and Y. S. Lincoln (eds), *Handbook of Qualitative Research*, Thousand Oaks, CA: Sage, pp. 324–39.
This is a chapter within the cited text, and covers participatory inquiry methods in sufficient detail for most students at this level. In addition, the *Handbook* itself is a rich source of material for anyone undertaking qualitative research.

REFERENCES

Ackoff, R. L. (1981) *Creating the Corporate Future*. New York: John Wiley.

Charette, R. N. (1995) 'No one could have done better', *American Programmer* July: 21–28.

Checkland, P. and S. Holwell (1998) *Information, Systems and Information Systems*, Chichester, Sussex: John Wiley.

Clarke, S. A. and B. Lehaney (1997) 'Total systems intervention and human inquiry: the search for a common ground', *Systems Practice* 10(5): 611–34.

de Olivera, R. D. and M. D. de Olivera (1982) 'The militant observer: a sociological alternative', in B. Hall, A. Gillette and R. Tandon (eds), *Creating Knowledge: A Monopoly? Participatory Research in Development*, New Delhi: Society for Participatory Research in Asia.

Ewusimensah, K. and Z. H. Przasnyski (1991) 'On information systems project abandonment: an exploratory study of organizational practices', *MIS Quarterly* 15(1): 67–86.

Foote Whyte, W. (1996) 'Emancipatory practice through the Sky River Project', *Systems Practice* 9(2): 151–7.

Hamlyn, B. (1993) *Report of the Inquiry into the London Ambulance Service*, London: Prince User Group Ltd and Binder Hamlyn.

Hirschheim, R. and H. K. Klein (1989) 'Four paradigms of information systems development', *Communications of the ACM* 32(10): 1199–1216.

Ives, B. and M. Olsen (1984) 'User involvement and MIS success: a review of research', *Management Science* 30(5): 5.

Lawrence, M. and G. Lowe (1993) 'Exploring individual user satisfaction within user-led development', *MIS Quarterly* June: 195–205.

Lin, E. and Hsieh, C.-T. (1990) 'Dysfunctional user behaviour in systems development', *Journal of Information Systems Management* (Winter): 87–9.

Lyytinen, K. and R. Hirschheim (1987) 'Information systems failures: a survey and classification of the empirical literature', in *Oxford Surveys in Information Technology*, vol. 4, Oxford: Oxford University Press, pp. 257–309.

Mintzberg, H. (1991). 'The effective organization: forces and forms', *Sloan Management Review* 32(2): 54–67.

Morgan, G. (1986) *Images of Organisation*, Beverly Hills, CA: Sage.

Mumford, E. and D. Henshall (1978) *A Participative Approach to Computer Systems Design*, London: Associated Business Press.

Mutch, A. (1996) 'The English Tourist Network Automation Project: a case study in interorganizational system failure', *Tourism Management* 17(8): 603–9.

Ormerod, R. (1996) 'Putting soft OR methods to work: information systems strategy development at Richards Bay', *Journal of the Operational Research Society* 47(9): 1083–97.

Reason, P. (1994) 'Three approaches to participative inquiry', in N. K. Denzin and Y. S. Lincoln (eds), *Handbook of Qualitative Research*, Thousand Oaks, CA: Sage, pp. 324–39.

Robinson, B. (1996) 'Limited horizons, limited influence: information technology experts and the crisis of the London Ambulance Service', *Proceeding of the IEEE* no. 4: 506–14.

chapter five

STRATEGIC ALIGNMENT

INTRODUCTION

This chapter is concerned with the alignment of corporate strategic management and information systems strategic management, which is seen to be more than a simple problem of selecting information *technology* to support the strategy of an organisation.

A strategic alignment model is presented as a framework for the process, which then progresses by means of determining the current status of an organisation's IS and IT planning (the 'IS map'), and analysing the business and IS domains of the organisation in *continuous alignment*.

Four strategic alignment perspectives are discussed, from which an organisation's strategic context may be determined, based on the type of organisation. Finally, a strategic action framework is presented, drawing together the strands of the strategic alignment problem in an action process, based on information needs analysis, and supported by techniques to model the business and information system domains.

LEARNING OBJECTIVES

This chapter will examine:

- the problem of aligning strategies for information management with an organisation's overall strategic management;

- a process for strategic alignment in practice;

- alignment perspectives, and their relevance to information systems strategic alignment;

- a strategic action framework, relating business and information systems strategies under the umbrella of information needs analysis, and models to support this.

THE ALIGNMENT PROBLEM

It is often assumed that the purpose of strategic alignment is to align information *technology* with an organisation's corporate and/or business unit strategies. However, such an approach has been challenged in recent years and cannot any longer be taken for granted. First, it cannot be assumed that all organisations *have* a corporate or business strategy, and if they do not – or at least if such a strategy is not written down – there is little with which to strategically align information technology.

Corporate strategy and the problem of IS strategic support

AJ Engineering* has been in business for over fifty years, and in that time has forged an enviable position for itself as the market leader in the UK supplying centralised suction pumps for office and domestic use.

The 1990s brought considerable changes to the suction pump market, with large multinationals entering into the supply of the smaller products which are the core of AJ's activities. The market, in the space of five to ten years, has become truly global and dominated by companies which are able to transfer products and information across national borders.

AJ's operation is underpinned by centralised information and control systems designed for internal efficiency to better service a known local market, but management recognises the need to

continued . . .

---

gain access to the wider, global markets in order not just to grow but to compete and survive. Nowhere, however, is this strategy documented, and at present neither the skills nor the will exist within the company to develop information systems able to support this as yet unwritten strategy. Aligning IT with the new corporate strategy is not an option, since the distance between them is too great, and AJ is losing the battle to compete in its market place.

* AJ Engineering is a pseudonym.

Furthermore, information technology cannot be viewed as distinct from the rest of the business, assuming that, once corporate strategy is detailed, a strategy for IT can be formulated to 'fit' the corporate strategy without regard to any other issues. Such an approach assumes a model of the organisation in which the corporate strategic thrust 'pulls' information technology support in its wake. But such a model will not fit all organisations. What of the technology-based organisation, where new technologies not only provide the new products, but also become ingrained in the processes used to make those products? Arguably, in such companies, technology, including information technology, drives the organisation's strategy.

What is proposed as an alternative is a strategic model (Figure 5.1) in which all the elements of corporate and information systems strategy are aligned, so that an organisation's information resource is placed to support that organisation's strategic and, ultimately, operational activity. Figure 5.1 illustrates this position.

Baets (1992) puts strategic alignment 'in a broader framework of information needs analysis (before even attempting the process of alignment) and not just [attempting] to align IS strategy into corporate strategy, but [defining] them in parallel'. Similarly, Venkatraman *et al.* (1993) argue that the strategic issues related to information systems have focused strongly on IT strategy and have seen it as 'a functional strategy that responds to the chosen business strategy'. This leads to a focus on internal issues such as the information architecture (dominated by types and configurations of computer equipment), processes and skills, and fails to deal with the opportunities which exist in the market place and may be exploited through IS strategy.

As is illustrated in Figure 5.1, the information need drives the process, whilst central to that process is the organisation's corporate strategy, together with the IS map: the framework of information systems currently

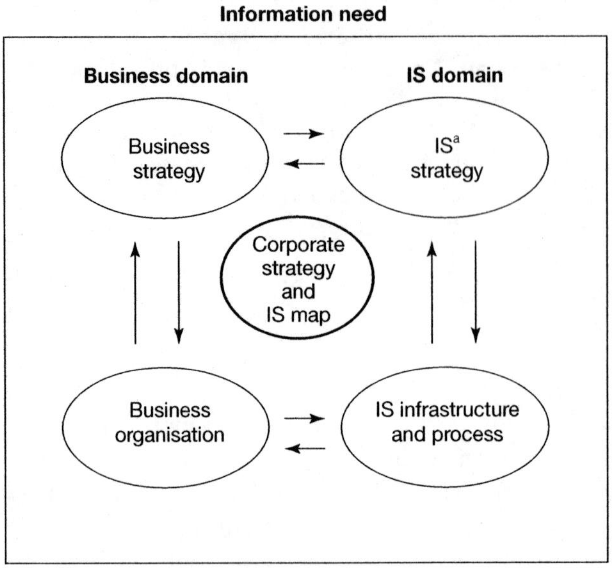

Information need

Note: [a] In the original model this appears as 'IT strategy'. IS is my interpretation.

Figure 5.1 **Extended strategic alignment model**

used to support organisational activity. Information needs are met through the business domain (business strategy and business organisation) and IS domain (IS strategy and IS infrastructure and processes) interacting to support the organisation.

CASE EXAMPLE

Strategy Formulation in UK Universities: The 'Value for Money' Study

In mid-1998, the Higher Education Funding Councils for England, Scotland and Wales and the Department of Education in Northern Ireland commissioned an 'Information Systems and Technology Management Value for Money Study', in which are outlined recommendations for formulating information strategic planning within higher education institutions (mostly universities) in the UK. The key findings of the study may be summarised as:

- Few institutions have a formal *information* strategy.
- Most have a formal *information systems* and/or *information technology* strategy.
- Few IS or IT strategic plans cover the use of IS or IT throughout the institution.

continued . . .

- Few IS or IT strategic plans link the use of IS or IT to the institution's overall strategic objectives.
- Some institutions have identified the financial and physical resources of the central IS or IT function, but none has a resource model for the institution's IS or IT provision as a whole.

In summary, the key objectives to emerge from this study are a need to:

- Align information strategy with the organisation's overall strategic mission.
- Enable planning and monitoring of IS and IT.
- Identify the resources necessary to deliver the strategy.

These recommendations have been used as the basis for strategically planning the information resource in the University of Hull. Strategic alignment was an important element of this strategic initiative, with an identified need to determine strategies for information, information systems and information technology, and to pursue the objectives and scope of the strategy within the context of the overall strategic objectives of the University. An Information Strategy Review Group (ISRG) was charged, during the period June 1996 to September 1997, with reviewing the existing IT strategy, which had come to the end of its term, and with laying the foundations of a wider ranging information strategy.

The first report of the ISRG stressed the need to develop a strategic approach to information management, examined the vital importance of the effective exploitation of information resources as a means of achieving the University's mission, and insisted that the introduction of new IT solutions must be preceded by a fundamental reappraisal of the information flows underlying the institution's key business processes.

A series of seven consultative workshops were then held to discuss the documents and to test their validity. These workshops involved a wide range of academic, academic-related and administrative staff of the University, and were extremely successful as a means of involving the University community generally. The discussions produced some valuable additional information, and there was general endorsement both of the analyses presented of the current situation and of the proposals for remodelling. The workshops had two practical outcomes: first, a set of recommendations for procedural changes was produced; second, a prioritised set of user requirement statements were generated that fed into the planning of the redevelopment of the student record system. These user requirement statements were implemented, in the majority of cases involving more detailed functional specifications produced by the information managers in consultation with users.

The University of Hull developed its information strategy alongside the development and implementation of its new corporate systems. Rather than being a

continued . . .

divergence from the intentions of the information strategy, they used the operational necessity of addressing the problems with their student records system to give an additional impetus to the development of their information strategy. The information strategy therefore developed from the experiences gained in the development of their new systems. They managed to retain the information strategy's emphasis on the information and embed this in their development process. This process can now be replicated in other areas of the University's activities.

(Source: HEFC, 1998)

In the universities' case example, the strategy process was seen to begin with a strategy for *information*. It is this 'information need' that lies at the centre of the approach to strategic alignment followed here. Unless the information need is established, progress cannot be made with any degree of confidence on IT or IS strategy, since there is no clear picture of what needs those strategies aim to fulfil.

So the alignment process may be visualised in terms of four essential elements: corporate strategy; business strategy; information systems strategy; and information technology strategy – all of which need to be kept in continuous alignment in the service of an overall information require- ment. This is essentially the approach recommended in two separate studies, first by Baets (1992) and later by Venkatraman (Venkatraman *et al.*, 1993), and which is represented by the composite model in Figure 5.1.

However, whilst this is a useful framework, it does not guide the process of strategic alignment. For this, a more detailed approach, based on this framework, is outlined in the following sections.

THE PROCESS OF STRATEGIC ALIGNMENT IN PRACTICE

Earl (1989: see Table 5.1) argues that organisations exhibit five stages of planning for IS, starting with a mapping of IT and IS resources to assess the coverage and quality of the technology and applications. Once the organisation gains confidence with this, attention moves on to an analysis of business needs in order to better direct the IS efforts. However, this stage often serves only to emphasise the poor quality of business planning, and thereby stunt the development of IS strategic plans. The third stage, Earl sees as 'messy [involving] a mix of detailed planning and investi- gation'. Essentially this involves bringing together the first two stages in a coherent planning approach. Stage 4, competitive advantage, is one which most organisations aspire to, but few attain: and even if attained, few are

Table 5.1 Planning in stages

Timeframe/factor	Stage 1	Stage 2	Stage 3	Stage 4	Stage 5
Task	IS/IT mapping	Business direction	Detailed planning	Competitive advantage	IT strategy connection
Objective	Management understanding	Agreeing priorities	Firming up the IS strategic plan	Finding opportunities	Integrating IS and business strategies
Direction/involvement	DP/IT lead	Senior management drive	Users and IS mainly involved	Executive management and users	Partnership of users, general management and IS
Methodological emphasis	Bottom-up survey	Top-down analysis	Matching top-down and bottom-up plus investigations and prototypes	Inside-out processes	Multiple methods accepted
Planning context	Inexperience/unawareness	Inadequate business plans for the purpose	Complexity apparent	Impatience	Maturity

(Source: Earl, 1989: 86)

able to sustain (see chapter six). Finally, the most successful organisations, argues Earl, reach a position where IS, IT and corporate strategy are integrated within a participative environment, encompassing users and managers within the organisation.

DETERMINING THE CURRENT STATUS OF IS AND CORPORATE STRATEGIC PLANNING IN THE ORGANISATION: THE IS MAP

This approach can be used by an organisation to determine its current position in relation to corporate strategy and IS. As with all classifications, it is important to realise that this represents 'ideal types', useful as an aid to thinking about the strategy process, but not to be seen as a pick list from which an organisation can choose its strategic position. For example, a too literal reading of Earl's work might lead the reader to the erroneous conclusion that different businesses or business units will be able to identify their position as 'Stage 1' or 'Stage 4', but this is not the case. In any organisation, the IS map, at any given time, will be a complex mixture of the above stages: the purpose of mapping is to attempt to map this complexity.

The business and information systems domain

Once the IS map is determined, attention can be given to other elements of the model (Figure 5.1), which is divided into business and IS domains. The business domain consists of business strategy and the business organisation or infrastructure, whilst the IS domain comprises IS infrastructure and processes and IS strategy. The arrows indicate the need for all elements of the model to be continuously aligned around corporate strategy and the IS map; and in satisfaction of the overall information need, it must be *continuously aligned*, since all the elements are ever changing. The strategic alignment process consists of two stages: first, determining an alignment perspective; second, undertaking the alignment process.

The IS map indicates the stage of planning that an organisation has reached, and rests on the idea that there is little point in, for example, expecting an organisation to strive to seek competitive advantage from IS if it has not achieved the understanding implicit in the previous three stages. The alignment perspective builds from the position determined by the map, and looks more at how strategic alignment can be pursued in the light of a particular organisational context.

The alignment perspective

The first difficulty facing an organisation is therefore that of determining the alignment perspective relevant to the business. Venkatraman *et al.* (1993) refer to four perspectives: strategy execution; technology potential; competitive potential; and service level, each of which focuses on a different section of the model (Figure 5.1). Strategy execution as a perspective (Figure 5.2) sees business strategy as the main driving force.

Strategy is formulated by management, and both organisational design and IS and IT are adapted to the changing business strategic needs. This is a very common approach to IS planning, but one which may be disastrous if used inappropriately. The current organisational design and the available choices of IS infrastructure to support the proposed strategies may, for instance, be so constrained that the strategic vision promoted by management may be simply unattainable.

Technology potential (Figure 5.3) focuses on available technologies and the infrastructure necessary to their success, with business organisation and business strategy following the technological lead. This is similar to the perspective above, but without the same constraining factors. The aim is to identify the best IS and organisational configurations needed to implement the chosen strategies, and the implication is that the organisation will have the necessary flexibility to achieve these.

Competitive potential (Figure 5.4) seeks to exploit emerging IT capabilities to generate competitive advantage, either by enhancing products or by improving processes, with business strategy being modified to take advantage of new IT opportunities. This approach, whilst appealing, may often fail to deliver the anticipated benefits, particularly if the

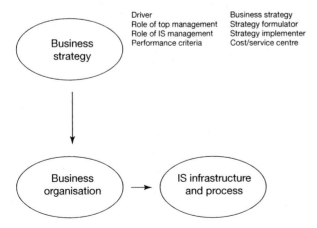

Figure 5.2 **A strategy execution perspective**

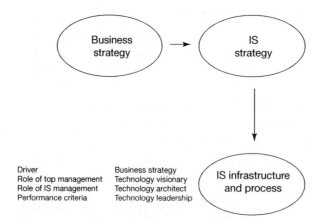

Figure 5.3 **A technology potential perspective**

Strategic alignment: a 'technology potential' perspective

EMIS Ltd supplies information systems solutions to UK universities: systems which encompass student monitoring, timetabling, examination scheduling, links to financial information packages, ad hoc reporting, and many other solutions. The application systems supplied are becoming the standard for universities that follow modular degree schemes, and are now in use at around one-quarter of all UK universities.

These systems enable universities to take advantage of technology potential in pursuing key strategic aims such as increased participation in higher education through a broader offering of courses, but they rely on universities being able to make use of a generalised application package.

Increasingly there is evidence that no two universities operate alike, and consequently the standard offerings from EMIS need to be adapted to the needs of different clients. Unless undertaken with care, a given organisation can be left with highly adapted systems which prove difficult to amend further or even maintain in the longer term. The technology potential is there, but it can be difficult to harness it where the business organisation or business strategy is strongly ingrained and inflexible.

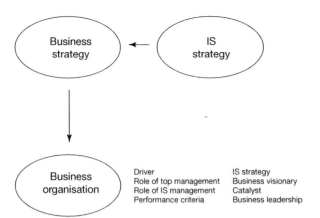

Figure 5.4 **A competitive potential perspective**

concentration is on IT rather that the information resource as a whole (see chapter six). The service level perspective (Figure 5.5) concentrates on IS strategy and IS infrastructure to produce an improved organisation. The danger here lies in becoming detached from the business strategy and losing focus.

The empirical and theoretical evidence therefore strongly supports the view that strategy in the 'information systems' domain should begin with a perception of the information needs of an organisation, and that information systems and information technology should be seen as supporting or supplying that need. Alignment of IT, IS, information and corporate strategies, the framework for which is encapsulated in

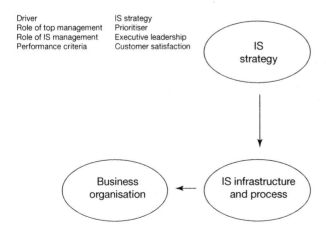

Figure 5.5 **A service level perspective**

Figure 5.1, then becomes a continuous process of aligning the business domain (business strategy and business organisation) with the IS domain (IS infrastructure and processes and IS strategy) in accordance with corporate strategy and the organisation's IS map. It has been argued that the alignment perspective relevant to the organisation must be determined, and that only then is the organisation ready to move on to implementing strategic alignment. This implementation is the subject of the next section.

STRATEGIC ACTION

Once IS mapping has been used to determine an organisation's alignment perspective, the strategic alignment model (Figure 5.6) lays out a framework for translating this into action. The stages of this process are iterative and the model enables that iterative process.

In principle, the process of strategic alignment consists of determining information needs for the organisation, and aligning the business and information systems domains in satisfaction of those needs. Whilst, as with any iterative model, the order of the activities is not prescribed, unless the organisation already has a clear definition of its information needs, the process would begin here.

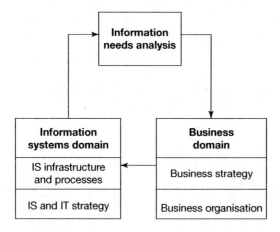

Figure 5.6 **The process of strategic alignment**

Information needs analysis

Information needs analysis is determined by reference to Figure 5.7. The aim is to assess information needs in relation to the organisation's external and internal environments and its values and objectives. This is

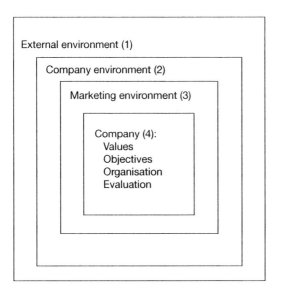

Figure 5.7 **Structure for corporate information**

Source: Adapted from Baets (1992)

an important and difficult part of the process, which must be approached systematically: the penalty for poor analysis at this stage will be the likely failure of the whole alignment process.

The external environment (1) consists of such things as the general economic climate, including interest rates, inflation and general political influences. Within this, the company environment (2) is more focused, detailing the economic climate in which the organisation operates. The classic approach to assessing the marketing environment (3) is SWOT and PEST analysis; in particular, the analysis of opportunities and threats, and of the political, economic, social and technical arenas in which the organisation is operating. Alternatives are, however, available, amongst which environmental scanning and especially 'gatekeeper' approaches are particularly relevant when dealing with technology. The principle of the latter is that the organisation designates 'gatekeepers' who continually appraise the use of systems within the organisation against developments outside. The company's internal policies and values (4) are the focus of the final part of information needs analysis. Each part of this analysis must be viewed in relation to the whole, and determining it demands a facilitated participatory process, the aim of which is to gain and improve understanding within the company.

international perspectives

The changing external and marketing environment of the motor industry

In the early twentieth century, Henry Ford pioneered mass production of cars with the Model T Ford, aimed at satisfying an almost insatiable demand for cheap transportation. Such was the external environment and market for this product that Ford was able to concentrate on internal issues such as the development of mass production techniques, sourcing components and financing each new venture.

Contrast this internal focus with the industry today. Over-supply and intense competition characterise this market in Europe, where four main players (Ford, General Motors, Volkswagen and Fiat) are battling for supremacy. The external environment demands attention to ecological issues such as pollution, over-use of fossil fuels, and moves to reduce traffic movements, particularly in and around major cities.

An understanding of these external and marketing environments is essential for any organisation competing for custom. Minor players such as Jaguar and Volvo have already been swallowed up – perhaps even the major organisations are no longer immune?

Analysis of the internal environment of an organisation is essentially about determining the balance of structure and culture, and is covered in more depth in chapter seven. In outline, currently available evidence points to a need for the internal environment to be viewed in both structural and cultural terms, with an over-concentration on structure at the expense of culture giving rise to tensions which prove difficult to resolve.

Information need is the basis of the whole process, and great care must be taken to determine those needs in relation to the organisation, its market and the wider environment. Since information to support this must be drawn from various parts of the organisation, the determination of information needs will be a highly participative process, demanding a human-centred approach.

The business domain

The second part of the process of strategic alignment involves gaining improved understanding of the business domain (Figure 5.6). The primary tool for analysing a company's internal business domain is Porter's value chain (Porter, 1990). Care should be taken when using this, however, to incorporate Porter's more recent ideas which cast the value chain as an integrated model, rather than as a collection of functional areas. Viewed in this way, information systems provide the links between the primary activities (inbound logistics, operations, outbound logistics, marketing and service) and the means of ensuring that support activities (infrastructure, human resources, technology development and procurement) are used to their full advantage. Increasingly, for example, in organisations using just-in-time manufacturing systems, procurement, inbound logistics and operations are linked by technology-based systems which ultimately control the whole manufacturing process. Care must also be taken to ensure that this analysis of the organisation fits the structural and cultural issues raised by the information needs analysis.

Structural and cultural conflict from information needs analysis

A well-known firm of professional accountants decided that information needs analysis was the key to improved efficiency and commissioned a study of information needs. The consultants, concentrating on administrative movements and paper flows, recommended a complete upheaval of existing practices to better fit the perceived need.

The change initiative was abandoned within a matter of months. Analysis had privileged structure ahead of culture, and the new practices were almost unanimously rejected by the accountants, who, over a period of years, had evolved complex work practices which were ingrained in their culture and which they were unprepared to change.

The consultants bemoaned the 'inflexibility' of accountants and proclaimed the benefits of their new systems to the end. But in the final analysis the consultants had failed to understand the deep-seated cultural traditions of their client, and by doing so had failed in their objectives.

Finally, within the business domain there will be the general corporate or business strategy, details from which must be extracted at this stage.

The information systems domain

Analysis of IS infrastructure and processes commences with an internal and external environmental audit, using the strategic grid (Figure 5.8) to summarise the current position. The strategic grid is a means by which the organisation's current and potential applications may be categorised according to their current or potential value. In practice, it has been found

STRATEGIC	HIGH potential
Critical to the business and of the greatest potential value	Potential value high but not confirmed
Essential for primary processes	Needed to support the business but of little strategic value
FACTORY	SUPPORT

Figure 5.8 **The strategic grid**

Source: McFarlan (1989)

that this analysis is more powerful if it is conducted in two modes: the 'is' mode, detailing where on the grid applications are currently seen to rest; and the 'ought' mode, assessing where the same applications *should be*. The power of this approach derives from a perceived weakness in analysing where applications *are*, in that this can serve to constrain their potential. By assessing where they *ought to be* an organisation is immediately beginning to define necessary changes.

Analysis using the strategic grid has been developed by the author's research and consultancy team over a number of years. The first stage of this analysis involves listing an organisation's IS applications and positioning them on the grid. New applications are becoming available all the time, and organisations should be aware of those which are new and untried, but which they should be at least reviewing and perhaps even sampling in use. These are the 'high potential' applications: they may succeed or they may fail; however, the key for any organisation is to gain understanding of them but, unless following a very high risk strategy, not to bet your business on them.

From the applications entering at the top right of the grid, those which prove successful will begin to move round in an anti-clockwise direction. Initially they enter the strategic segment, where any company which is not beginning to use a given application will initially be left behind by its competitors. This happened in the UK insurance industry in the 1990s, when Direct Line pioneered telephone-based insurance, cutting out the intermediary brokers. Though competitors have extensively copied this approach, Direct Line still maintains its market lead today.

> **Internet retailing in the food industry**
>
> In some sectors of the economy, such as book or record retailing, sales over the internet are already big business. As yet, this revolution has had little impact in one of the largest sectors – food retailing.
>
> There is no technical reason why this should be so. Computer software exists which, across the internet, would allow the customer to browse the shelves of a supermarket, choose and pay for products. In addition, parts of the process would be immeasurably improved: repeat purchases of branded goods would be simplified; and imagine being able to submit a shopping list to a range of supermarkets, and ordering only from those with the lowest price on an item-by-item basis.
>
> Clearly both the retailers and the customers have a lot to think about, and neither is yet ready to make the necessary changes to facilitate these new approaches. But from the retailers' point of view this is an emerging, high potential application, and therefore one with which they must be ready to proceed when their competitors do.

Arguably, the IS used to support Direct Line's activities, which was initially a strategic use of an emerging technology, has now moved to the 'factory' quadrant: the take-up has been so great that all major players in the market depend on it for their primary processes and would therefore not survive without it. Lastly, as applications age and lose their value as a strategic weapon, they may continue for a time in a support capacity, but should be selectively divested and replaced by systems selected from the emerging and pacing quadrants. It is here that many organisations are most at fault, hanging on to dying systems, often through fear of change: perhaps even Direct Line should be considering the possibility that one day the systems which are now such a fundamental part of its business will be no more than support applications?

So much for the IS, but what of the IT so often used to enable it? Technology which is used to support IS typically will have a finite life. This begins with the emergence of an as yet untried technology, moves through a phase where major competitors are sampling it, to a position where an organisation will not survive without it, and a final scenario where keeping the technology too long makes the company uncompetitive. In effect, the technology life cycle mirrors the application life cycle outlined above.

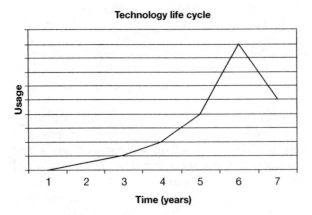

Figure 5.9 **The technology life cycle**

In any given industry, it is essential to be aware of currently used technologies in these terms. Figure 5.9 shows the life cycle of a typical technology, where the first year is one of emergence, followed by periods in which a company in the industry must increasingly commit to the new technology in order to compete, before moving out of it and into newer technologies as its impact declines. Of course, many technologies, after early promise, will fail to make an impact, so companies must be equally ready to dispose of these once their potential proves unrealisable.

Little (1981) provides an approach to monitoring new technologies by superimposing them on the strategic grid (Figure 5.10). Information

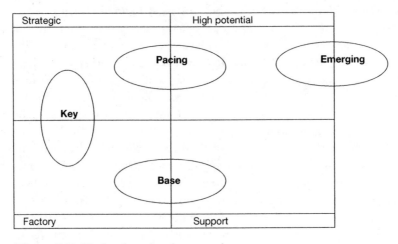

Figure 5.10 **Technology implementation**

Source: Little (1981)

technologies support strategy as enabling mechanisms, the aim being to find the correct technologies to enable the required IS and corporate strategies to be achieved.

The grid can be used to match existing technologies against applications and to plan the introduction of future technologies. As with applications, technologies enter the grid at top right, and proceed round in an anti-clockwise direction. The principle of this analysis is that emerging technologies need to be used for systems which have high potential but which are not critical to the business, and must be carefully monitored until a decision to utilise them can be made; pacing technologies should be invested in selectively for applications in which competitors are investing. Primarily the aim is to decide which are likely to become key, at which point they must be used in building strategic/factory systems; base technologies should be selectively divested.

External monitoring feeds this process, which will not succeed unless the organisation has a clear view of what technologies are relevant to its operations in any of the quadrants at a particular time. A generic view of IT at the present might see, for example: internet and multi-media technologies as emerging; wide area networks as pacing; local distributed systems as key; and central computers with terminal access as base. Finally, as with the strategic grid, it is important to review technology usage in terms of what *is* happening and what *ought to be* happening, with the normative (ought) position being of primary importance in planning future systems.

In summary, the objectives of application portfolio and technology management are:

- to conduct internal and external audits to determine the current position regarding applications used and the technology used to support them;
- to use the audits to determine the applications and technologies available to the organisation;
- to classify applications according to the strategic grid (Figure 5.8): this should be done for both current and intended or available applications;
- to determine the available technologies, categorised as emerging, pacing, key or base (Figure 5.7);
- to match current applications and technologies to those available.

New technologies fundamental to the development of information systems are emerging all the time, and one factor which must not be overlooked in setting IS strategies is the extent to which such strategies are dependent on this emergence. Internal and external environmental scanning must therefore be a continuous process.

CONCLUSIONS

Strategic alignment studies are concerned with the problem of managing the strategic development of information systems so that it is 'aligned with' corporate strategic management. This is a complex problem, which cannot simply be approached by writing a corporate strategic plan and then developing the necessary IS, or even worse IT, to 'support' that plan. All the evidence, both empirical and theoretical, indicates that corporate strategy and information strategy should be developed in a complementary fashion; this is done in this chapter under the umbrella of information needs analysis.

A process is presented for strategic alignment in practice, including techniques for determining an organisation's current position, and developing *continuously aligned* business and IS strategies. The alignment perspective, which helps in understanding an organisation's context of application, is presented as part of this process.

Finally, a framework for strategic action is given, driven by information needs analysis and incorporating models to support strategy development and alignment within the business and IS domains.

In all the available literature, both theoretical and empirical, and in all the cases with which I have been involved, this level of understanding is gained only through extensive participative study. Baets (1992) discusses the use of operational research techniques, soft systems methodology, socio-technical systems design, or the viable systems model. Recent research and practice shows this to be a limited view, and suggests a multi-methodological approach, involving a fundamental understanding of the process of action research (see chapter four) to underpin the participative activities.

SUMMARY

- The alignment 'problem' in the domain of information strategy has frequently been wrongly cast as a need to align *information technology* with corporate strategy. Recent evidence points to the corporate, business and information domains all requiring to be continuously aligned within information needs analysis.
- The process of strategic alignment begins with an analysis of the organisation's information needs. This must then be related to the internal and external business and information systems domains of the

organisation. For information systems and information technology analysis, the strategic grid (Figure 5.8) and the technology implementation grid (Figure 5.10) have been identified as valuable analysis tools.

- The alignment process must be continuous and must align the business and IS domains with corporate strategy. The means of undertaking this process are seen to depend on participative study, based on soft methods and the findings from action research.

REVIEW QUESTIONS

1　How might the IS map of an organisation be determined?

2　What are the stages in the process of information needs analysis?

3　What are the principles behind the analysis of applications and technologies?

DISCUSSION QUESTIONS

1　TM Graphics is a design consultancy undertaking vehicle design for the US car industry. The equipment used for this is computer-based and high technology, but it is used by professionals who are working to support the strategies of their client companies. In terms of the model in Figure 5.1, what alignment perspective might be relevant to such an organisation?

2　Determining an organisation's information need may be seen as fundamental to the strategic alignment process. How might this task be undertaken?

3　It has been argued that the alignment process is fundamentally concerned to align corporate strategy and information needs. Where do IS and IT fit into this process?

---

case exercise

Otis Elevator (Loebbecke, 1992)

Otis Elevator is a global elevator company, operating from head offices in France. It has only one family of products – elevators and escalators,

continued . . .

associated with which are two activities: new equipment and service. The new equipment business is in turn made up of sales, manufacturing and construction, whilst the four types of services are contractual maintenance, repair, modernisation and replacement.

Otis's major existing applications in the mid-1980s consisted of:

- *OTISLINE*, a centralised, customer service centre which operates 24 hours a day, seven days a week. Over time, Otis customers started to consider OTISLINE as a new industry standard. OTISLINE keeps a record on each lift;
- the *Customer Data Base* with more than 40,000 customers stored, used by sales and marketing;
- a *'Remote Elevator Monitoring' (REM) system*, recently introduced by Otis North America, which utilises microchip technology to monitor an elevator and automatically notify Otis if it is malfunctioning. The major market for REM is France, where more than 7,000 units are implemented. In other European countries, only a few hundred REM systems are installed, while in the US Otis North America has not sold any;
- *for internal process*, Otis was still using a system that was developed in the early 1960s.

The Otis information systems 'master plan' called for five new applications (SAGA, SALVE, STAR, SAFRAN-N,S,K and SAFRAN-O) to be implemented between 1986 and 1992.

SALVE will be a support system to be used by sales representatives in their negotiations with the customer from the initial contact to the booking stage. Once the order has been booked it will be passed to SAGA, a contract management system. The information gained from SALVE and SAGA will serve as input for STAR, the purchasing and supplier management system. SAFRAN-N,S,K will handle invoicing and other accounting functions, and SAFRAN O the billing of maintenance services.

From the information given, assess the scenarios facing Otis using the strategic and technology implementation grids. Make an assessment in both 'is' and 'ought' modes.

FURTHER READING

Baets, W. (1992) 'Aligning information systems with business strategy', *Journal of Strategic Information Systems* **1**(4): 205–13.

Earl, M. J. (1989) *Management Strategies for Information Technology*, London: Prentice-Hall.
Earl is a key author on IT and IS strategy, although his earlier work should be approached with caution as it now seems to over-emphasise IT at the expense of the overall information or IS position.

Porter, M. E. (1990) *The Competitive Advantage of Nations*, London: Macmillan.
This book contains reference to Porter's work on organisational analysis, including the value chain.

Venkatraman, N., J. C. Henderson and S. Oldach (1993) 'Continuous strategic alignment: exploiting information technology capabilities for competitive success', *European Management Journal* 11(2): 139–49.
This paper and Baets (1992) contain the source information on which the strategic alignment model and analysis is based.

REFERENCES

Baets, W. (1992) 'Aligning information systems with business strategy', *Journal of Strategic Information Systems* 1(4): 205–13.

Clarke, S. A., B. Lehaney and S. Martin (1998) 'A theoretical framework for facilitating methodological choice', *Systemic Practice and Action Research* 11(3): 295–318.

Earl, M. J. (1989). *Management Strategies for Information Technology*. London: Prentice-Hall.

Galliers, R. D. and A. R. Sutherland (1991) 'Information systems management and strategy formulation: the "stages of growth" model revisited', *Journal of Information Systems* 1: 89–114.

Higher Education Funding Councils (HEFC) (1998) *Information Systems and Technology management Value for Money Study: Management Review Guide*, London: UK VFM Steering Group, HEFC Value for Money Initiative.

Little, A. D. (1981) 'Technology implementation', in J. Ward and P. Griffiths (eds), *Strategic Planning for Information Systems*, Chichester, Sussex: John Wiley.

Loebbecke, C. (1992) *Staying at the Top with Otis Elevator: Sustaining a Competitive Advantage through IT*, Fontainebleau, France: Insead-Cedep.

McFarlan, F. W. (1989) 'Portfolio approach to information systems', in B. W. Boehm (ed.), *Software Risk Management*, Washington, DC: IEEE Computer Society Press, pp. 17–25.

Porter, M. E. (1990) *The Competitive Advantage of Nations*, London: Macmillan.

Venkatraman, N., J. C. Henderson and S. Oldach (1993) 'Continuous strategic alignment: exploiting information technology capabilities for competitive success', *European Management Journal* 11(2): 139–49.

chapter six

COMPETITIVE ADVANTAGE FROM INFORMATION SYSTEMS

INTRODUCTION

The idea that information systems can be used to give an organisation an advantage over its competitors came to the fore in the 1980s and spawned a number of studies purporting to show how new and developing computer technologies such as databases and networks could be applied to give an organisation a competitive edge.

The foremost author in the field of competitive or 'strategic' advantage is undoubtedly Michael Porter, and initially his ideas on how to generate competitive advantage will be used as a basis for this chapter. As these ideas are developed, however, using contributions from other authors, it becomes clear that the idea of competitive advantage from information is a far from simple one. The first question to emerge concerns whether competitive advantage can be generated from information technology or whether, primarily because the concern at this level is with the *use* of the technology, focus should be on information systems, or even more generally simply on information. Second, studies in this domain seek to determine *sustainable* competitive advantage, and questions have been raised concerning the sustainability of a competitive advantage based on information. Finally, there is the question of whether such competitive advantage could ever be systematically planned, or whether it is, at the extreme, just the product of chance.

LEARNING OBJECTIVES

This chapter will examine:

- the conceptual and empirical background to competitive advantage;

- the possibility of generating competitive advantage from information technology, information systems, or information;

- the value of seeing organisations as systems;

- the sustainability of competitive advantage from information;

- the potential for planning to achieve competitive advantage from information.

PORTER'S THREE GENERIC STRATEGIES

Michael Porter is probably the best-known author in the field of competitive strategy. In terms of its relevance to information systems, one of Porter's key notions is that of generic strategies. He proposes (Porter, 1990: 39) that competitive advantage is to be gained from one of three generic strategies: differentiation; cost leadership; and focus. Differentiation means making your product or service in some way different from that of your competitors; cost leadership generates an advantage by producing at a lower cost, and thereby increasing profit margins; focus is the concentration on a particular area of the market where the organisation aims to outperform competitors by its increased knowledge and skills.

In attempting to generate competitive advantage from information systems (IS), a number of authors have concentrated on these generic strategies, with cost leadership and differentiation being the most favoured approaches. Cost leadership, for example, has been the dominant use of technology by the UK banking sector, using such approaches as automated banking to reduce the overall cost base, which largely consists of personnel costs. The use of information to differentiate has been applied, for example, by insurance companies to differentiate the offering of an

CASE EXAMPLE

Tesco Supermarkets and Differentiated Strategy

In 1994, Tesco was the second largest supermarket chain in the UK, having consistently lagged behind the more successful Sainsbury chain: Tesco needed a strategy which would move it to number one and keep it there. By 1998 this had been achieved through a strategy of differentiation in the service offered.

Essentially, the products sold by Tesco and Sainsbury are the same, though historically Sainsbury had always maintained a reputation for better quality, with Tesco being founded on a 'pile it high, sell it cheap' approach. Tesco attacked this perception through a carefully crafted series of improvements in customer service. These varied from simple customer care strategies such as escorting 'lost' customers to the required product rather than just directing them, to the pioneering of loyalty cards, whereby all customers earn 1 per cent of their purchase values as a bonus to be spent in the future.

At present, whilst not only Sainsbury but all other major supermarket chains are emulating this approach, Tesco is maintaining its position as leader in the market by a strategy of continuous service differentiation initiatives.

essentially service-based product. In the UK this has resulted, in the ten years leading to the new millennium, in an increasing migration away from high street based insurance agencies towards telephone-based organisations such as Direct Line (see Chapter 5). However, before looking at examples and theoretical evidence based on the work of Porter and others, it might be helpful to discuss competitive advantage in relation to IT, IS or just information.

COMPETITIVE ADVANTAGE FROM INFORMATION TECHNOLOGY, INFORMATION SYSTEMS OR INFORMATION?

It is important to distinguish between IT, IS and information, the difference between them being illustrated in Figure 6.1.

Information passes between individuals and groups in a given social environment. In terms of the subject of this book, the social environment will constitute all or part of a business organisation. Information within an organisation may therefore be seen as the 'superset' which information systems and information technology are used to support. An information system then may be seen as any system which better enables information to be passed within this environment. The relevance of such a view is that such a system is not necessarily a technological one, but may take many forms.

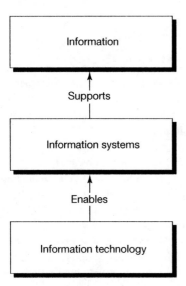

Figure 6.1 **The nature of information technology, information systems and information**

A system for controlling vehicle production

Vauxhall Motors, in common with all leading multinational mass-produced car manufacturers, uses highly sophisticated computerised robot assembly methods at its Luton, England, factory to produce the Vauxhall Vectra. The changeover from Cavalier to Vectra production involved a complete transformation from previous assembly methods, requiring a new production line, some 300 or more new robots, and the implementation of a 'just-in-time' system whereby component supply is linked to production with the key aims of minimising stocks whilst continuously improving quality.

The success of this change has been nothing short of outstanding; it has involved the use of a number of new information systems, one of which is required to track the flow of components from original supplier, into the Luton plant, and through the whole production process to final assembly into the finished vehicle. A number of approaches to this were considered, many of which involved the use of sophisticated computer technology, but eventually the decision was taken to control component usage through the production process by means of a 'Kanban' system.

continued . . .

This involves the use of hand-written stock cards attached to the component 'bins', which are updated every time stock moves. The information system in this case therefore consists of a relatively simple card system which, when combined with the knowledge and experience of those using and managing it, becomes a key part of the overall production process. Information technology plays no direct part in this system, but there is no doubt that this is an information system which is critical to the production process.

The impact of this view of an information system should not be underestimated. First, its purpose is to support the information needs of the organisation (see chapter five), and it is therefore cast as a 'soft' or human-centred issue. Second, the conceptual or theoretical background underpinning this study is not technological, but is based on theories of social systems.

Organisations as systems

Organisational or business systems are open, human activity systems which display the properties of: boundary; emergence; holism; interdependence; hierarchy; transformation; and communication and control.

First, why are they open systems? Well, 'open' means open to the environment, and the alternative is to see them as closed, or not affected by the outside environment. Since a business system must be impacted by events beyond its own boundary (political decisions, competitors and so on), it cannot be viewed as closed.

Second, why human activity systems? This question is fundamental to an understanding of the role of information technology and relates back to the 'hard/soft' debate discussed earlier in the book. A business is a collection of individuals, or a social group, gathered together for a purpose. The activities within a business are therefore carried out in support of this human activity, and whilst the technology (whatever it may be) can be seen as in support of this activity, it can never be viewed as an end in itself.

The concept of a system without a boundary is meaningless, since it is essential to determine what lies inside and what lies outside the system. All systems exhibit emergence, or emergent properties, which are only evident when there is a complete system in operation. For instance, a car is made up of components which by themselves do not provide a means of transport: this only emerges once the components are combined into a system. Systems therefore need to be viewed holistically, since their purpose is often only evident if the system as a whole is considered. Systems consist of sub-systems which are interdependent, between which there is communication, and which are arranged in a hierarchy of sub-sub-systems and so on. Finally, all systems perform a transformation process which must be controlled.

The place of information technology is now clear. It may be used to better enable the information system to function, which in turn assists with information planning within the organisation. However, by itself IT serves little purpose.

CASE EXAMPLE

Nene University College, Northampton, UK: A System for Managing Student Information

Nene is one of just over a hundred university sector institutions in the UK. In common with almost all such organisations in the early 1990s, it was faced with the problem of managing rapidly growing undergraduate numbers, which by 1998 had reached around 7,000.

Nene's solution was to commission an information system for this purpose, but as the project progressed, they found the boundaries widening.

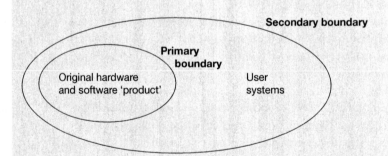

Originally, the project was conceived in terms of a product based on a single database, with a clearly defined user base having access to this central information through computer terminals connected to a central computer. However, it soon became clear that there were other advantages to be gained. One example of this is shown in the figure, where, according to the original project, user systems, such as the systems used to maintain student attendance and assessment records, were not to be catered for. In effect, in systems terms, they fell outside the 'technical' system

continued . . .

boundary, but were nevertheless one of the sub-systems which would interact as part of the overall system of student monitoring. As the project progressed, it was decided to bring these user systems inside the primary boundary, developing them (using the Excel spreadsheet) to interact with the central database software.

The system had been perceived not as a technical one, but as a system for managing student information, and this perception significantly enhanced its overall utility.

How, then, is competitive advantage to be generated from the use of IT? Practical and theoretical evidence from the literature will now be assessed to determine this.

Information technology

The concept of competitive advantage from information technology is an appealing one. In a common-sense way, it seems obvious that, if your organisation can get its hands on some relevant new technology ahead of its rivals, it must gain a competitive edge. From the earliest studies of competitive advantage from information technology, however, doubt has been cast on this concept. Clemons (1986), for example, follows the generic categories of Porter (cost leadership, differentiation and focus) to throw light on these issues. His view is that, by concentrating on internally or externally focused applications, an organisation can gain advantage by means of reduced costs or by differentiating the product through improved delivery times and the speed of servicing customers.

Competitive advantage from information technology: the problems of use and sustainability

The general consensus view from studies conducted to date seems to be that competitive advantage cannot be gained from information technology, but only from its use. This is an important issue, since it places the competitive advantage debate firmly within the realms of information or information systems, not information technology.

Following on from this argument is the problem of whether competitive advantage can be sustainable. If concentration were placed on competitive advantage from IT, then the sustainability question becomes one of how an organisation can continually

continued . . .

update its technology to maintain its advantage. However, if competitive advantage comes from the use of information, sustainability lies in an organisation always being better at this than its competitors, which is attainable even where all competitors in an industry have the same technology, and is a product of the human activity in the organisation, not the technology.

Weill (1990), however, argues that such advantages are not simply IT-based, but derive from the way in which an organisation *uses* the technology, and cites claimed examples of competitive advantage from IT, primary among which is the SABRE booking system of American Airlines and the similar APOLLO system of United Airlines. Weill argues that these are examples of strategic advantage being gained from IT investment, but that such gains will not necessarily follow from all such investments. Weill's research is indicative of the train of thought that developed through the 1980s, which increasingly pointed towards a concept of competitive advantage which is not simply IT focused, but which was seen to depend on the use of the technology within the overall strategic and operational aims of the organisation. As will be seen below, this development has continued into the new millennium, often citing the same or similar practical examples.

Information systems

Adcock *et al.* (1993) refute the suggestion that competitive advantage may be obtained from information technology:

> Max Hopper, vice-president of information systems at American Airlines . . . refutes the view that SABRE increased American Airlines' marketing edge over rival airlines . . . American Airlines doesn't worry whether the competition has access to the technology because American thinks it can be smarter in how it uses the technology.

This argument is supported by the fact that both American Airlines and Baxter Healthcare, another major example of IT use for competitive advantage, were happy to sell their IT applications to competitors, thereby gaining revenue from the sale whilst maintaining their competitive advantage by better use of the technology through superior product and service offerings. From these and other examples of the use of IT in enabling competitive information systems, Adcock *et al.* conclude that, although short-term competitive advantage from IT is possible, in the longer term the impact of IT is on industry structure rather than the competitive position of any particular organisation within that industry.

---

international perspectives

Competitive advantage from information systems: the networking organisation case study

In 1998, three organisations, The Networking Firm, Procall, and the University of Luton, combined in a joint venture to offer a service which uses converging technologies to aid corporate transformation. The core of the product is Procall's already operational call-centre technology, which is used by a wide variety of organisations to provide a front-office function to often widely dispersed organisations.

The difficulties encountered by many organisations, however, have little to do with the technology, but a great deal to do with its use. Typically, those most successful in this respect are young companies which currently have an under-developed front-office function, as is the case with a client which consists of a number of international consultants who have no office base: they use the technology to provide a virtual office, whilst the consultants remain contactable by telephone, fax or email wherever they are in the world.

To achieve these results for existing companies, the new joint venture offers a diagnostic trial of the technology, combined with consultancy and education as required. Initial feedback suggests a significant demand for this kind of change programme, focused on human and organisational rather than technological issues.

Information

It seems clear that, through the last twenty years of the twentieth century, the focus for competitive advantage moved away from IT and towards IS, highlighting the use made of the technology within a given organisation rather than just the technology itself. It appears that both IT and IS need to be integrated into an organisation, and that it is the organisational system which should be the focus of attention. In citing Baxter's Health-care as gaining advantage from the 'service behind the system', Adcock *et al.* (1993) argue that competitive advantage does not come from IT or IS, but from the 'underlying management processes' which make use of them. These are human activity processes, and need to be seen in terms of systems, including the information system to be implemented and its place in the wider organisational system of which it is a part. The purpose is to facilitate the use of information within an organisation, if necessary through the use of an IT-enabled information system.

THE SUSTAINABILITY OF COMPETITIVE ADVANTAGE FROM INFORMATION

The question of competitive advantage sustainability can now be placed in perspective. Any such sustainability is essentially short-term in nature and related to such issues as the time taken to 'harvest' the results, and switching costs (costs incurred by competitors switching to the new technology, or customers switching from one supplier to another) (Clemons, 1986). In so far as competitive advantage is derived mainly from the technology used, its sustainability will depend on continuing innovation in order to stay ahead of the competition as they imitate the organisation's lead, or innovate to move ahead themselves. This innovative use of IT is therefore, in the long term, unsustainable and will soon be lost (Adcock *et al.*, 1993). Competitors are quick to respond: what happens is that the industry structure as a whole changes, as was evidenced, for example, with the switch of the banking system to automated teller machines.

The greatest promise of sustainability comes from human advantages. If the system of concern is seen in terms of a human activity system, then sustainability perhaps depends on a holistic view of interdependent sub-systems which, when functioning together, give rise to advantages which competitors find hard to emulate. Such advantages may be intangible, relying on such things as the skill base of the organisation, experience of those involved, adaptability and so on.

CASE EXAMPLE

Loyalty Cards and the Sustainability of Competitive Advantage in UK Retailing

In the mid-1990s, Tesco, now the largest supermarket chain in the UK, introduced loyalty cards. These are individual cards held by customers through which are recorded all the transactions made by that customer, and which return to that customer 1 per cent of the total value of purchases made. In addition, some products are sold with 'bonus points' attached to them (for example, an extra 100 points with a bottle of wine), each point being worth one penny.

continued . . .

Initially, Tesco gained customers from this initiative, but it was quickly copied by all the other major supermarket chains, so that by 1998, all were offering a standard 1 per cent loyalty bonus together with occasional extra bonuses. Consequently it is now arguable whether there is any actual competitive advantage to be gained by any one retailer; rather the structure of the industry has changed.

The current decision by some of these retailers to cease loyalty cards and move to other initiatives, such as 'permanently low prices', further supports the view that competitive advantage is not sustainable. As a colleague of mine has commented: 'I think loyalty cards are an excellent idea – I am loyal to all of them!'

PLANNING FOR COMPETITIVE ADVANTAGE FROM INFORMATION

The conceptual and empirical evidence above points to significant questions concerning whether organisations can *plan* to gain competitive advantage from the implementation of information systems and at the very least suggests that sustaining such an advantage is not possible. Sustainable advantage seems to derive, not from the technology or systems themselves, but from the way in which they are used, which once again indicates the primacy of human issues over those of technology or even applications. Nowhere is this message more emphatic than in the empirical studies of Adcock *et al.* (1993), which contribute compelling evidence that organisations must concentrate on the effective use of IT and IS, in line with the objectives and goals of the organisation as a whole. In strategic terms, it seems more important to align IT and IS strategies with the overall business strategy, an issue covered in chapter five, than to concentrate specifically on gaining an elusive competitive advantage from such systems. The message seems to be not to plan for competitive advantage from information, but to strategically manage information more effectively and accept the advantage this gives.

FRAMEWORKS FOR THE ANALYSIS OF COMPETITIVE ADVANTAGE

Regardless of the view taken concerning the sustainability of competitive advantage or its attainability from IT, IS or information, any organisation needs to understand its competitive position. Porter (1991) mounts a convincing argument to support the view that an organisation's success depends on its competitive position relative to others in the same industry or sector, and offers a number of frameworks to help assess this. Although these frameworks are geared to competitive advantage overall, rather than just competitive advantage from information, they can be adapted for the latter purpose. Similarly, Earl (1989: 54) discusses the use of business strategy frameworks. These approaches are adapted here to provide an overall method for analysing and managing an organisation's competitive position in respect of information.

Although competitive advantage is not seen to be derived from IS or IT in isolation, nevertheless there is a need to determine what information systems and technology are being used by competitors, what is available, how these systems are used, and when they should be changed. The importance of human-centred issues in this process makes this even more critical: human activity systems take time to adapt and change, giving rise to a need to manage the process of IT and IS infusion in an organisation.

Three key approaches may be seen as supporting the monitoring and management of competitive advantage from information in an organisation: industry or sector analysis; positioning the organisation within the industry or sector; and internal analysis of the organisation.

Industry or sector analysis

In terms of the information it uses, a firm needs to position itself within its industry or sector. Porter and Millar (1985) have devised a framework for assessing this. The importance of this analysis is that the value of information management to an industry needs to be assessed, and competitive advantage from information is more critical in companies where information content of the product and information intensity of the value chain is higher.

---

international perspectives

Oil industry exploration: information intensity in prospecting for a low information content product

In the early part of the twentieth century, a young J. Paul Getty was in a car with his father, driving through California. As the car continued across a seemingly flat landscape, it began to labour, and the Gettys became increasingly excited at the realisation that they were actually driving over a bulge in the terrain.

'There is oil here,' commented father George Getty. 'Let's get out and stake a claim.' The early days of oil prospecting abound with such stories, true or otherwise, but one thing is not in doubt: Getty oil grew from such humble beginnings to become a major international oil company and was sold to Texaco in 1982 for $10 billion,

continued . . .

then the largest corporate take-over in history – at which time it was still owned by the Getty family.

Now, as we enter the new millennium, things have changed a little. The latter part of the twentieth century saw the theory of continental drift replaced with the theory of plate tectonics, according to which the earth's crust is made up of a number of plates which are continuously moving in relation to each other (hence earthquakes and volcanoes at the margins of the plates). When oil was formed from dead forests, plates which were then adjacent may now be hundreds or even thousands of miles apart. But the oil can still be found by looking at magnetic fields in the rocks, and inferring which rock formations were adjacent at the time of the formation of the oil.

The information necessary for oil prospecting has come a long way in a hundred years.

Positioning the organisation within the industry

The position of an organisation within its industry will also help determine its approach to information management (The five forces model: Porter, 1990). Where rivalry is strong, organisations can use information to keep pace with or remain ahead of competitors, as is the case with the earlier-cited airline booking systems, now used by all major airlines. The threat of new entrants can be reduced by barriers to entry such as the high cost of acquiring and using the necessary information systems: the lower the cost of acquisition, the greater the need to be better at using them. The threat of substitutes implies a need for information about the nature of substitute products or services, and indicates an area where information management is likely to be crucial. Suppliers' and buyers' positions are best managed through information on the supply and customer chains, a strategy adopted by all the major car manufacturers.

Internal analysis

The value chain is often interpreted as a very functional view of the organisation, breaking it down into five functional areas (inbound logistics, operations, outbound logistics, sales and marketing, and service), overlaid by activities which span them (human resource management, procurement, firm infrastructure, and technology development). However, Porter (1990) stresses the importance of the 'drivers' of competitive advantage, key among which are linkages between activities and the sharing of information between activities. These linkages require co-ordination, and the whole value chain must be managed as a system.

Seen in this way, the value chain becomes a valuable technique for assessing the importance of information to the organisation. Information may be seen as pervading and linking all the activities in the value chain, with culture (HRM) and structure as important elements, enabled by available technologies.

By combining the information intensity matrix, the five forces model and the value chain, an organisation can therefore assess the relevance of information to its operations; the need for enhanced use of information to combat the external forces to which its operations are exposed; and the value of information in linking and enhancing internal activities. Before concluding this chapter, I want to turn, in the next section, to empirical evidence from the competitive advantage domain.

INFORMATION AS A STRATEGIC RESOURCE

Earl has conducted a number of cross-sectional and longitudinal studies of the use of IT among chief executive officers (CEOs) and chief information officers (CIOs) of major corporations, a summary of which may be found in Earl and Feeny (1994). Earl's summary of the views of CIOs points to the need for IT to be viewed as an asset which can contribute to the overall strategic advantage to be gained from the use of information in an organisation.

The chief findings are that CEOs are 'polarised between those who see IT as a strategic resource and those who see IT as a cost', whilst the CIO's key task comes down to changing attitudes by adding value from IT implementation. Whilst remaining unhappy about the 'confusion' of IS and IT in this study, it is hard to disagree with the general direction of thinking. Loosely cited, Earl is seen to advocate that the successful business has no information, IS or IT strategies, only business strategies.

CONCLUSIONS

In terms of its information resource, an organisation clearly stands to gain from the strategic use of *information*. Focus on IT alone, or even on IS, seems unhelpful: the real competitive advantage comes from the *use* of technology and systems. There is clear evidence from empirical studies that, even where a number of major players within an industry have access to the same technology, some succeed by using that technology better, while others fail. To quote from Max Hopper, American Airlines succeeds by being smarter in the use of the same technology. Sustainability comes from the interaction of interdependent sub-systems within a system of human activity: this kind of competitive advantage is not 'planned for' in any instrumental sense, but is the natural outcome of information that is strategically managed.

SUMMARY

- Competitive advantage from information is placed in a conceptual framework initially based on Porter's three generic strategies: differentiation, cost leadership and focus.
- It is argued that sustainable competitive advantage cannot be gained solely from IT, but depends on how the technology is used. This argument is seen to be strongly supported by the available empirical evidence, which demonstrates competitive advantage being sustained by organisations against competitors who have access to the same technology.
- The view of organisations as systems is introduced to reinforce the evidence pointing to a need to look not only at IT, IS or information, but at the organisational problem context 'holistically'.
- A number of frameworks for the analysis of competitive advantage are then presented, and suggestions made for combining them to assess the relevance of information to its operations; the need for enhanced use of information to combat the external forces to which its operations are exposed; and the value of information in linking and enhancing internal activities.
- A view of information as a strategic resource is outlined, again offering significant empirical support to the IT/IS/information debate.

REVIEW QUESTIONS

1 What are Porter's generic strategies? How are they applied in gaining competitive advantage from information?

2 Is it possible to generate *sustainable* competitive advantage from information technology? What is the empirical evidence?

3 How can the sustainability of competitive advantage from information be generated?

DISCUSSION QUESTIONS

1 'Technology enables an organisation to differentiate its offering from that of its competitors.' To what extent do you believe this to be true, and if true, how would such an advantage be sustained?

2 The example of Nene College might be seen as supporting the view that, in assessing competitive advantage, organisations must be viewed as systems. Discuss this proposition, using examples from your own experience.

3 The frameworks available for assessing competitive advantage suggest it cannot easily be planned. Do you agree with this statement? If *planning* for competitive advantage is not an option, how is the issue to be approached?

---

case exercise

The American Airlines SABRE system (Adcock *et al.*, 1993)

SABRE, an online reservation system using terminals and personal computers placed in the offices of travel agents, raised American Airlines' revenue through increased ticket sales and special royalty payments from other airlines. Contrary to the view that the competitive advantage achieved was attributable to IT, Max Hopper, vice-president of information systems at American Airlines, pointed out that, although it is dangerous to ignore the power of information technology, it is more dangerous to believe that, on its own, even an *information system* can provide an enduring business advantage. He refutes the view that SABRE increased American Airlines' marketing edge over rival airlines and called such claims groundless. He referred to the existence of equivalent rival systems (for example, United Air Lines' Apollo System) and the fact that any dissatisfied travel agent can remove the SABRE system and replace it with another system in as little as 30 days.

American Airlines has sold SABRE's revenue management capabilities to all interested customers since 1986 because it was felt it had more to gain by selling the system than by keeping it to itself as secret proprietary knowledge. The company's goal is not to build computer systems, but to lead in applying technology to core business objectives. American Airlines doesn't worry whether the competition has access to the technology because American thinks it can be smarter in how it uses the technology. The huge systems owned by United Air Lines and American Airlines are virtually identical, and small companies as well as TWA, Texas Air, Alaska Airlines and Delta Air Lines all offer computerised reservation systems.

What do these examples tell us about competitive advantage from IT? From the literature, what is the supporting and counter evidence for this view?

FURTHER READING

Adcock, K., M. M. Helms and W.-J. K. Jih (1993) 'Information technology: can it provide a sustainable competitive advantage?', *Information Strategy: The Executive's Journal* **9**(3): 10–15.

Clemons, E. K. (1986) 'Information systems for sustainable competitive advantage', *Information and Management* **11**: 131–6.
This paper and Adcock *et al.* (1993) cover admirably the issues concerning the possibility of gaining and sustaining competitive advantage from information, and begin the separation of IT, IS and information developed in this chapter.

Earl, M. J. (1989) *Management Strategies for Information Technology*, London: Prentice-Hall.
The chapter in this book on 'Information technology and strategic advantage' is a must for any student of this topic.

Porter, M. E. (1990) *The Competitive Advantage of Nations*, London: Macmillan.
This book is the starting point for any student of competitive advantage. My only other recommendation in this regard, for those with a love of the historical context, would be to read Adam Smith's *Wealth of Nations*.

REFERENCES

Adcock, K., M. M. Helms and W.-J. K. Jih (1993) 'Information technology: can it provide a sustainable competitive advantage?', *Information Strategy: The Executive's Journal* **9**(3): 10–15.

Clemons, E. K. (1986) 'Information systems for sustainable competitive advantage', *Information and Management* **11**: 131–6.

Earl, M. J. (1989) *Management Strategies for Information Technology*, London: Prentice-Hall.

Earl, M. J. and D. F. Feeny (1994) 'Is your CIO adding value?', *Sloan Management Review* **35**(3): 11–20.

Porter, M. E. (1990) *The Competitive Advantage of Nations*, London: Macmillan.

Porter, M. E. (1991) 'Towards a dynamic theory of strategy', *Strategic Management Journal* **12** (Winter): 95–117.

Porter, M. E. and V. E. Millar (1985) 'How information gives you competitive advantage', *Harvard Business Review* July/August.

Weill, P. (1990) 'Strategic investment in information technology: an empirical study', *Information Age* **12**(3): 141–7.

chapter seven

STRUCTURE, CULTURE AND CHANGE MANAGEMENT IN INFORMATION SYSTEMS

INTRODUCTION

Organisational structure and culture are fundamental factors to be considered in information systems strategic management (ISSM).

In this chapter, organisational structure is classified according to Mintzberg's 'forces and forms': as this classification was made to support studies of corporate strategy, it is seen to be particularly relevant to the study of ISSM. The problems of organisational culture are then outlined. A model for the components of culture is presented, and the relevance of this to organisational analysis discussed.

These issues are drawn into the analysis of strategic change management, which is then related directly to ISSM. A process for IS change management is detailed, leading to an overall change management framework (see Figure 7.4).

LEARNING OBJECTIVES

This chapter will examine:

- the importance of different approaches to structure and culture in organisational analysis;

- the relationship between organisational structure and culture and information systems;

- change management from structural and cultural perspectives;

- a framework for information systems change management.

ORGANISATIONAL STRUCTURE AND CULTURE

Although discussion of organisational structure and culture is commonplace, there is little agreement on how the variety of structures ought to be classified. Bureaucratic, hierarchical, matrix and other structures appear regularly in the literature, but offer little help to those wishing to determine the different types of organisation in order to match some aspect of organisational practice to given organisational forms. To the strategic thinker this has been particularly limiting: strategy cannot be formulated and implemented independently of the type of organisation concerned.

Jackson (1987) argues that we should use the metaphors of organisation developed by Morgan (1986) as a basis for taking alternative views of organisations, and looks at four particular views: organisations as machines, organisms, cultures and coercive systems. A mechanistic view sees organisations as machines, within which rule-based systems can be used to control operations in a deterministic environment: that is, one in which, if the inputs to the process are known, the outputs can be predicted with a high degree of certainty.

Seeing an organisation in 'organismic' terms is to take a systems perspective. The organisation is a combination of sub-systems interacting together and attempting to maintain a 'steady state' within their environment. Organisation as culture rests on the view that the primary consideration in any organisation is its functioning as a social structure.

> **'Hard' systems thinking: a mechanistic view of oil refining**
>
> Crude oil is delivered to refineries for processing. The core of an oil refinery is a 'hydro cracker', which chemically processes the crude into its various products (heating oil, diesel, petrol, aviation fuel and so on). As with many highly mechanised and technologically complex processes (nuclear power and robot manufacture are two further examples), the fundamental aim is to design a machine that will perform the task with minimal human intervention. There is little doubt that much of the industrial progress of humankind has rested on such an approach, and we should not underestimate the value of the achievements made. However, such an approach reaches its limits when the complexity of human activity is added to the system of concern.
>
> What is acceptable for an oil refinery has been tried in social contexts and found wanting. The message is clear: if your organisational problem situation is characterised by high levels of human activity, the value of a mechanistic view is severely limited.

This view helps explain the functioning of business for which there is no discernible structure, such as the ad hoc collection of individuals in some advertising agencies who join together only on the basis of business opportunities. Finally, organisations as coercive systems sees them as functioning according to power structures, introducing a radical element into the debate by challenging the power structures, which is not evident in the other three views, that promote essentially a perspective of organisations supporting the status quo or maintaining existing power structures.

This classification can be helpful in information management, where certain types of approach have been argued to fit against certain views of organisations. So, for example, hard systems thinking matches the mechanistic metaphor, organisational cybernetics the organismic metaphor, soft systems the cultural metaphor, and critical systems the coercive metaphor. However, whilst Jackson's work lays a foundation for *understanding* the structure/culture conflict in organisations, it is Mintzberg who has provided the primary classificatory framework.

ORGANISATIONAL STRUCTURE

According to Mintzberg (1991), organisations are subject to seven forces: direction, proficiency, innovation, concentration, efficiency, co-operation and competition. By direction Mintzberg is referring to the strategic direction or vision of the organisation. Efficiency is the cost-benefit problem, seen for example in re-engineering initiatives, which aim to reduce cost by re-engineering the existing process in a more efficient way. Proficiency relies on knowledge and skill and is seen, for example, in firms of solicitors or accountants. Concentration is the requirement for certain parts of the organisation to concentrate their effort, for example on specific markets. Innovation covers the requirement to adapt and to learn about changing circumstances, such as by discovering new products. The forces for co-operation and competition which lie within the pentagon, Mintzberg sees as catalytic, and related to culture: co-operation is 'The pulling together of ideology'; competition rests on conflict.

These seven 'ideal types' of forces seen to dominate organisations have been used to define seven 'ideal type' forms of organisation, a classification which contributes to an understanding of organisational structure and also helps to relate this more directly to the cultural issues. The organisational forms are: entrepreneurial, professional, machine, diversified, adhocracy, ideological, and political. By looking at what would happen if one particular force dominated an organisation, each of the organisational forms can be related directly to the forces, argues Mintzberg. So, for example, the 'machine' organisation is seen to be dominated by a drive for efficiency.

Structure/culture conflict in the professional adhocratic organisation

A common classification ascribed to higher education institutions such as universities is that of 'professional adhocracy'.

Disparate groups of professional academics join together at different times for various purposes, with much of the development of the organisation being dependent on these ad hoc groupings. So, for example, one academic may spend a single day working on an undergraduate teaching programme, an international research project and an internal management initiative. Within the space of a few hours this will involve working with three quite distinct groups of people, located in different parts of the world, and having different objectives.

continued . . .

> This adhocratic culture must be matched by a supporting structure, otherwise the whole system may fail to function. Commonly this means that physical structure (location of offices, lines of supervision) becomes less important, and 'virtual' structures such as electronic communication and shared internet sites are used.

The argument to be drawn from this is not that any one organisation will match neatly any one of the forms and forces defined, but that by using a model such as this a better understanding can be reached of the mix of forces which are affecting a given organisation and the structural mix that it might need in order to deal with that. In particular it may be possible to identify where structure and the forces affecting the organisation are in conflict and from there to move to a point where conflictual culture is incorporated in order to determine where tensions may exist within the organisation which it is possible to correct.

Mintzberg counsels against becoming too attached to any given configuration within an organisation. So, for example, the machine organisation can become so concerned with efficiency that innovation and proficiency suffer and when required are unable to gain a foothold. What is needed in any organisation is 'the dominance of a single force but also the constraining effects of other forces'. Managing this apparent contradiction is the structural problem that faces organisations.

In this chapter, these forms of organisations are used to help understand information management. Views of culture can further contribute to an understanding of the structural nature of organisations.

ORGANISATIONAL CULTURE

Culture may be seen as something which can be designed and manipulated, or something inherent within an organisation which can be understood and described, but which no one group (for example, management) is able to control. The way in which it is seen is critical to an understanding of how culture affects the management of information.

Organisational culture has been described as the collective will or consciousness of an organisation, composed of a pattern of beliefs shared by all its members. This view has given rise to the idea that culture can be created or manipulated and, further, to the concept that such manipulation is the preserve of management. Such a view relies on culture being seen as a unifying force within an organisation: something which drives towards consensus or emphasises organisational stability. But this emerges as a narrow concept of culture that does not do justice to alternative and equally valid and valuable conceptualisations. It also gives rise to a number of problems, among which are the question of how collective will could be empirically tested; how, if culture is a unifying force, do we have the cultural divisions evidenced in strikes?

The idea that culture can be created and manipulated by management is at best questionable. Culture emerges from the social interaction of all organisational members – managers are as much a part and product of the culture as all other members; they are not a privileged group standing proud of the culture and managing it.

In information systems, culture therefore needs to be understood so that an organisation is in a better position to incorporate information strategies which are in line with the existing culture and any cultural change seen to be in progress. A view of management as the only group effecting cultural configuration and change is not helpful. The organisation needs to determine what its 'culture' is, how it is changing, and where the major influences are coming from.

This essentially emergent view sees culture as embedded in the symbols, myths, ideologies and rituals of the organisation (Figure 7.1). Symbols are the shared codes of meaning within the organisation; they may appear as language (particularly evident in information technology), corporate offices, company car schemes, logos, or simply stories about the organisation that are passed down over the years. Myths are evident in all organisations, commonly appearing as founder myths or creation myths:

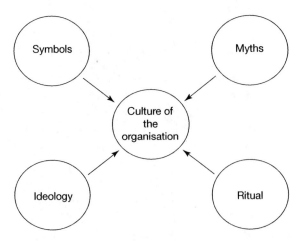

Figure 7.1 **The components of organisational culture**

J. Paul Getty was a self-made billionaire (actually his father was a wealthy lawyer who invested in oil and left over $15 million, a fortune in the 1930s). The ideology is an organisation's systems of knowledge or set of beliefs about the social world, key among which will be the ethical position. Too often, organisations are seen to have one ideology, but actually all organisations have sets of consonant and conflicting ideologies: in UK hospitals, the twenty years leading up to the new millennium have seen a period of increasing competition and capitalism which has been espoused by management, but arguably the dominant ideology of the care workers within those hospitals is little changed. Rituals within organisations help to cement the underlying values. Most sales conventions have acceptable behaviours, dress and so on which are not prescribed, but are known and followed: wear a suit and tie; clean your company car; support some speakers and not others.

Symbols, myths and ritual in the Digital Equipment Corporation

From its formation in 1957 until the late 1980s, the Digital Equipment Corporation (DEC) enjoyed over thirty years of uninterrupted success, ultimately brought to an end by the personal computer boom of the 1990s, which effectively destroyed the bulk of DEC's mini computer market.

The company offices were utilitarian, with no particular privileges in terms of space or quality of fittings being accorded to managers. Anyone entitled to a company car had a standard allowance, which he or she could add any amount to in order to upgrade. In fact, many senior managers drove company cars which had a much lower specification than those of their subordinates. The company founder was said to have started DEC in his shed, making computers to order, and to have expanded rapidly based on technological innovation.

DEC did not abound in ritualistic behaviour and appeared to all within it as an egalitarian organisation.

The brief review of structure and culture outlined here, together with its relevance to information systems, gives a basis for a discussion of the relationship of change management to information systems strategy. Change management, implicitly if not explicitly, underpins the domain of information strategy: formulating and implementing strategies for improving the use of information in organisations inevitably implies some form of change.

MANAGING STRATEGIC CHANGE

Information systems strategic change management has been dominated by methods which aim to plan and control the change process, examples of which, in the last thirty years, have been total quality management (TQM) and business process re-engineering (BPR). This has had the effect of privileging process and structure within an organisation ahead of people issues: in other words, TQM and BPR aim to alter the structure of the organisation and the processes which make up its activities, whilst the people within the organisation have to adapt to these new conditions (for a summary, see Cao *et al.*, 1999).

CASE EXAMPLE

Business Process Re-engineering

Consider a company which has dispersed sales and distribution locations. The company originally had separate manual sales systems at its various corporate locations. When an order was received, it was taken on a paper invoice and then sent to a local credit clerk. The clerk then determined the creditworthiness of the customer before the order was filled.

The company integrated IT into its credit checking functions by developing a database that allowed salespersons, in an on-line environment, to evaluate the creditworthiness of customers and authorise shipment. The database was expected to produce faster order fills, increased sales and customer satisfaction. The database also allowed them to re-engineer their sales process and save hundreds of thousands of dollars in personnel, training and hardware costs by establishing a centralised credit-processing facility.

Months after the system was in place, the company found that sales had dropped at several locations and uncollectable billing had risen at many others. Upon examination, they found many of the sites had unique seasonal and cultural factors that made local analysis of creditworthiness necessary. Unfortunately, the expertise of their ex-credit clerks was no longer available to the corporation, making the change process irreversible. The lifetime of specialised local credit experience that was stored in these clerks was very costly to replace.

There was also a marked increase in voluntary turnover of many of the organisation's sales representatives. Some salespeople expressed a general feeling of increased uncertainty in job requirements, that is, task ambiguity, and others resented the added duties associated with the new sales process. Many of the salespeople resisted the change in the sales process. Some of the company's best salespeople even left the firm and took their client bases with them.

continued . . .

In terms of the anticipated rewards from decreased costs and increased efficiency, the BPR of the company's sales process was a success. However, decreased sales, increased employee turnover and bad debt had an adverse effect on its current revenues. It is important to realise that the firm carried out IT-enabled BPR to achieve radical rewards but may have failed to recognise the full extent of the related process risks involved. The popular press is full of the testimonies of consultants touting the incredible productivity gains possible with BPR, but there seems to be a quiet void concerning the effects of failed BPR projects.

(Source: Fiedler et al., 1994)

TQM, it has been argued, has little to say about how to implement change successfully where people have different interests and values (Jackson, 1995), assuming, as it does, a common culture throughout the organisation. BPR offers a series of tools for identifying the necessary change and rebuilding the organisation in a new image. However, it has been suggested that BPR has little to say about problems beyond organisational processes: 'If re-engineering fails, no matter what the proximate cause, the underlying reason can invariably be traced to senior managers' inadequate understanding or leadership of the re-engineering effort' (Hammer and Champy, 1993: 213).

To counter these process- and structure-based approaches, research on change as cultural diversity has been increasing (Milliken and Martins, 1996). This varies from demographic diversity, such as race, gender and ethnicity, to more task-related dimensions such as functional specialisation and organisational level. It is suggested that effective cultural diversity management will encourage more creativity, better problem-solving and flexible adaptation to change, keeping the company ahead of the competition through mutual learning among organisational members. Methods suggested to manage cultural diversity include training (awareness training and skill-building training), mentoring (coaching, protecting, supporting, counselling), and technology mediated teams (designing teams and team meetings to make use of the myriad choices of technology available, such as electronic meeting support systems, video, e-mail and fax).

This background leads McKay (1997) to contend that the dominant views of change, including TQM and BPR, are based on 'manipulative assumptions about change', taking a planning approach within a largely structural framework. It is contended that such views ignore more recent developments which see change not as altering the past towards a new vision of the future, but rather of understanding the beliefs that have given rise to the current organisation and addressing those beliefs which underpin corporate culture. To overcome this view, researchers and practitioners began to incorporate people issues in terms of resistance and how to overcome that resistance: in effect, still perceiving the ability to plan a way through the cultural maze. Tactics for reducing resistance include education, communication, involvement and appropriate performance measures. Kudray and Kleiner (1997) display a commitment to the 'planning' approach in the observation that: 'Managers, including managers of change, need to remember that they are changing, manipulating, and re-arranging a variety of both human and non-human elements.'

What emerges from this school is the strong commitment to a cultural rather than a structural (manipulative) view of change. McSparran and Edmunds (1996) refer to survey evidence which points to culture being the primary consideration for managers undertaking change strategies. A cultural view places participation and communication as important elements of the change management process, but care needs to be taken not to neglect the other issues. In order to be successful, organisations need to manage *both* evolutionary and revolutionary change. Tushman and O'Reilly (1996) cite the semiconductor industry as an example of where both types of change have taken place over a relatively short period. In this industry, whilst culture is seen to be significant, failure to invest in new technologies or picking the wrong technology are equally significant reasons for failure. Where organisations have failed to adapt, failure can be traced to people within the organisation being unable 'to play two games simultaneously'. The argument is that typically, as firms grow, if they rely in the short to medium term on emergent strategies without undergoing any fundamental changes to structure, culture or people, the evidence suggests that eventually they will die. The cause is the cultural inertia that comes from the shared values, expectations and stories within organisations that have been developing over a long period. Failure to change the organisational culture can lead to failure of the organisation, as in the case of IBM quoted in chapter two.

Consequently managers have two perhaps seemingly conflicting objectives. The first is the need to manage in the short term by aligning strategy, structure and culture through periods of emergent strategy or incremental change. The second is the need to manage in the long term, which may require a transformational change, destroying what has seemed to be the core of the organisation's success: but this must be in the longer term, since such major changes in structure require that the organisational culture be given the necessary time to adapt and change.

To summarise, change management is dominated by 'manipulative' assumptions, with cultural factors, through which an organisation

CASE EXAMPLE

Cultural Change at British Airways

By 1981, British Airways (BA) was a failing company, posting multi-million pound losses. It had gained a reputation as the major international airline with the worst service. The solution to this was seen to be a change in staff culture.

BA, refocusing on service rather than transportation, developed a culture change programme: two days for employees; five days for managers. Almost all of the work force of nearly 40,000 were put through this course, which was supported by a system of evaluation and compensation through bonus payments.

The outcome has been, following a successful flotation on the stock exchange in 1987, the evolution of BA into one of the world's leading international airlines, renowned for its good service. By 1995 BA had behind it a solid record of profit in an era when most international airlines were posting losses. Sir Colin Marshall, Chairman of BA, continues to push the corporation towards a high-quality, personal service. The cultural change programme has been supported by the ongoing and proactive elimination of operational weaknesses, and by customers being encouraged to report problems, which BA then strives to solve quickly.

addresses the underlying beliefs which give rise to its response to change, being given insufficient attention. Early approaches to dealing with human issues, in which the beliefs of participants were seen as barriers to be overcome, have partially given way to a cultural perspective through which change is perceived as a participative rather than a planned process.

The most recent evidence suggests a need to combine methods aimed at dealing with change from both planning (revolutionary or transformational) and incremental (evolutionary) perspectives. In particular, whilst evolutionary change is valuable in the short to medium term, planned, revolutionary change may be necessary in the longer term, and may be inhibited by an ingrained evolutionary or incremental culture.

STRATEGIC CHANGE AND INFORMATION SYSTEMS

Early approaches to change facilitated by or involving information systems tread the familiar path of a structured or planned method. However, as in the general domain of change management, attitudes towards the management of change in information systems are altering significantly as we move into the new millennium. Even where a structured view is seen to be still relevant (Ryan, 1992), and business process re-engineering is advocated, the conclusion is reached that, whilst the processes are simple to re-engineer, difficulty is still encountered in getting the people involved to accept the change that comes from this. Orlikowski and Hofman (1997) see the traditional approach to change in organisations as one which starts with a plan and then manages the change according to that plan, with any alterations being matched by changes to the plan. This, however, conflicts with empirical evidence, which sees change rather in terms of progressing towards a more general objective, making changes in response to the conditions met along the way, often in an ad hoc fashion. Orlikowski and Hofman argue that there is a difference between how people think about change and how they implement it, which is very closely aligned to the Mintzberg view that people talk about strategies in one way and implement them in another. The emergent or incremental approach is seen to be particularly relevant when implementing new technologies, particularly open-ended and customisable technologies such as computer networks. Increasingly such technologies are used as general-purpose tools which the end user may customise and utilise in quite different ways across an organisation. Since the technologies to be implemented and the organisational impact of those technologies is not predictable, a planned approach is not seen as feasible. What is required is an approach to change which allows for emerging needs, unanticipated outcomes, continuous innovation and learning within the organisation.

By building on Mintzberg's (1987) emergent strategies, Orlikowski and Hofman have developed a model to deal with change in these circumstances which blends anticipated, emergent and opportunity-based change. Although the sequence is not defined, typically the implementation of new technology will involve an early anticipated stage, which over time then brings about further emergent and opportunity-based change in an iterative fashion.

Drawing on MIT's 'Management in the 1990s' programme, Benjamin and Levinson (1993) see the bias towards technology, rather than 'managing changes in process and organisational structure and culture', as a fundamental cause of IT benefits not being realised. A move is proposed away from what is seen as the traditional way of managing change through a management hierarchy, to an 'informated organisation' within which all have access to information and are empowered to use it. Once again this emphasises the multi-dimensional nature of change management, in this case transferred to the IT field.

Information systems change management, it seems, like strategy, is something we talk about one way and do another. Ask most people how they manage IS change, and they will talk of a plan or programme as though it is a fixed set of processes to achieve a known goal. Observe IS

Information systems networks and change management

One of the major IS changes in organisations over the last ten years has been the trend towards distributed networks of personal computers. The typical approach to implementing these is simple: turn the development into a technical problem, define the technical solution (number of personal computers, linkages, network software and so on), and implement the system.

Unfortunately, this ignores a fundamental factor in such networks: they are there to enable people to work together more effectively. The 'information system' in this case is explicitly *not* a computer system – the computers are there to enable the information system to work more effectively, but the system is essentially one of human activity.

Change in such an environment is therefore wrongly cast if viewed as technological, for which a solution can be engineered. The major change necessary is a cultural or social change in working procedures and habits, and failure to recognise this has caused the failure of many such projects to meet their objectives.

---

change management, however, and it appears as a much looser framework within which unforeseen circumstances have to be accommodated. As with organisational change management, anticipated, emergent and opportunity-based change must be managed together.

TOWARD A FRAMEWORK FOR INFORMATION SYSTEMS CHANGE MANAGEMENT

Positioning the organisation

Studies by Argyris and Schon (1974) suggest that organisations must determine their position on the grid (Figure 7.2), the aim being to move towards the bottom right.

This emphasis on positive attitudes to change, and to wide participation in the change process, further supports the cultural view and emphasises the value of learning in the change process. A widely suggested approach is to establish a core team, adopt a flexible approach and establish ad hoc structures such as task forces, of which the membership and appointment processes are key issues in establishing their credibility.

Decision-making

		Restricted to the management team	Extensive – involving all those affected
	Negative	Little learning or change	Anxiety-creating behaviour
Attitudes to change			
	Positive	Learning and change possible only if not dependent on other people	Learning and change possible

Figure 7.2 **Determining the organisation's change position**

Source: Argyris and Schon (1974)

Monitoring organisational effectiveness

A matrix for monitoring organisational effectiveness in change situations is proposed by Carnall (1990). The grid (Figure 7.3) maps efficiency and effectiveness on the horizontal axis, against quantitative and qualitative measures on the vertical axis. Carnall contends that organisations concentrate on the top left of this grid, focusing on profit and market share objectives through the control of costs. However, it is in the bottom half of this grid that focus is needed for IS strategy, particularly in the use of new technology through the softer resource issues of satisfaction and commitment.

Blocks to change

Also important in this respect is the need to identify blocks to change (Adams, 1987). Perceptual blocks can be a problem, one example being institutionalised blocks, such as an unwillingness to change the way things are done. If left, these blocks can have the effect of watering down the change which takes place, leaving a situation where the old methods continue within the new framework, with the benefits of neither being realised. To unblock needs open management, free expression and a willingness to discuss negatives as well as positives. Argyris (1985) stresses this as the need for 'open confrontation of issues'.

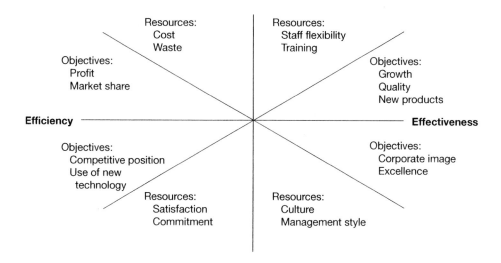

Quantitative measures

Resources:
Cost
Waste

Resources:
Staff flexibility
Training

Objectives:
Profit
Market share

Objectives:
Growth
Quality
New products

Efficiency ——————————————————————————— **Effectiveness**

Objectives:
Competitive position
Use of new
technology

Objectives:
Corporate image
Excellence

Resources:
Satisfaction
Commitment

Resources:
Culture
Management style

Qualitative measures

Figure 7.3 **Monitoring organisational effectiveness**

Source: Carnall (1990)

Change styles

Three styles are seen to be important (Boddy and Buchanan, 1992): imposition; education and communication; and participation. Whilst imposition might be seen as possible through a manipulative approach to change, the other styles clearly need to be supported through a participative framework.

People need help in coping with change: 'People need to understand the new system if they are to understand their own part in it' (Carnall, 1990). The problem here is that openness and confidentiality do not go well together, and organisations need constantly to seek ways of maintaining this balance. Many advantages are cited for involving people (improved decisions, better understanding and so on). The keys to this are flexibility, team building, networking, communication skills (stimulating motivation in others), and the ability to take a holistic view.

'Human performance in an IT environment is as much a social and organisational accomplishment as a technical one' (Boddy and Buchanan, 1992). The social context of the change is an issue of major importance. Care must be taken that organisational issues do not provide a major barrier to success, with thought needing to be given in particular to the organisational structure required to capitalise on, for example, new information systems.

These approaches to managing strategic change can now be drawn together into a framework which pays heed to the nature of change and change management, and to the particular requirements of the IS domain (Figure 7.4).

The process begins by positioning an organisation on the Argyris and Schon grid (Figure 7.2), determining the balance between attitudes to change and the decision-making process. So, for example, it may be determined that, whilst decision-making in the organisation is highly participative, attitudes to change are negative and are reducing the impact of the change initiatives. Here the difficult task exists of altering attitudes to change – the organisational culture.

The situation is then further informed by moving on to an assessment of organisational effectiveness. Implementation of new information systems frequently concentrates at worst on the top left of the Carnall grid (Figure 7.3) or at best on the bottom left. In such circumstances, thought needs to be given to how staff flexibility and training and the organisational culture and management style might be brought into the equation. Within this analysis, blocks to change can be addressed, although removing them might prove more difficult than imagined. For example, the way in which things are done in an organisation become institutionalised and difficult to change, but it must be changed if the organisation is to progress.

Depending on the analysis of the organisation's position, a change style can be chosen, normally a mix of imposed/planned and participative. More often, unfortunately, the analysis serves to illustrate problems in the organisation's approach to change, but management proves unwilling to submit to the necessary corrective action. Such a situation is highlighted in the case example.

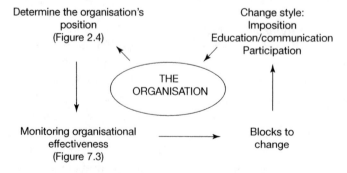

Figure 7.4 **A framework for IS change management**

CASE EXAMPLE

Implementing a Document Image Processing System at Eastshire District Council *

Eastshire District Council's (EDC) planning department maintains records of some 40,000 private and 5,000 business properties within its catchment area, together with up-to-date records of occupation and payment of local taxes.

Records are updated daily, and amount to some 500,000 transactions per annum. In 1995 a decision was taken to change the manual filing and paper management system used for this to one based on document image processing, whereby all paper records coming into the department would be scanned as a picture into a computer and managed from a computer network.

Under the old system, paperwork received was photocopied and sent to the relevant department for records to be amended and for filing. The new system replaces this with computerised documents, accessible to all who need to use them.

In terms of the framework in Figure 7.4:

1 The organisation has centralised decision-making with positive/negative attitudes to change (Figure 2.4).
2 Concentration in terms of organisational effectiveness (Figure 7.3) is strongly focused in the top left quadrant, with an emphasis on cost reduction.
3 Blocks to change are significant, with highly institutionalised procedures.
4 The change style chosen was one of imposition.

From the beginning things started to go wrong. Scanning proved to be a laborious business, taking much longer than expected, with the effect that staff who were poorly trained and even less motivated were working on incomplete records. Department managers began to superimpose manual procedures over the DIP system to 'paper over the cracks'. By 1998, after significant computer upgrades, training and considerable rewriting of procedures, Eastshire was effectively back to using the original system, with DIP supporting it as a very expensive filing system.

* Eastshire is a pseudonym.

CONCLUSIONS

An understanding of organisational structure and culture is fundamental to information systems change management. The identification of different forms of organisations and the forces that drive them helps to determine the relevant approach to IS, but this must be adapted according to the culture of the organisation, particularly where professional and adhocratic forms are in evidence.

The lessons from theory and practice counsel against a strongly structural approach to IS change management, with the focus predominantly on technology, and suggest that human activity factors be given more weight.

The proposed framework for IS change management takes account of these issues and approaches the problem from a mainly human perspective, which IT serves as an enabling technology.

SUMMARY

- Organisational structure is classified into five types (machine, entrepreneurial, professional, adhocratic and diversified) and the forces driving each type are discussed. The components of organisational culture are then mapped (symbols, myths, ritual and ideology) and related to information systems and change management.
- Approaches to managing strategic change are discussed, and are seen to be dominated by a structural view of organisations (for example, business process re-engineering, total quality management). However, alternatives are identified which privilege culture ahead of structure (for example, cultural diversity). These ideas are taken forward into a discussion of information systems change management.
- Information systems change management is shown to have relied mostly on structural views, where planning the process dominates. This is exposed as an impoverished position which evidence from the emergent school of strategy is seen to further question. The outcome is the idea of pursuing IS change management through frameworks for understanding rather than fixed, structural plans.

REVIEW QUESTIONS

1 What are Jackson's and Mintzberg's classifications of organisations?

2 What are the components of culture? Draw a cultural diagram for any organisation of your choice.

3 If change management is approached from a perspective of BPR or TQM, what does this say about the nature of the change process undertaken?

DISCUSSION QUESTIONS

1 Information systems change management must take account of the structural form of the organisation studied. Discuss the pros and cons of developing a fixed change plan for a professional/adhocratic organisation.

2 Some authors see culture as something to be manipulated, others see it simply as ingrained in the 'fabric' of the organisation – contained in its employees and managers. Why does this matter in IS change management?

3 Contrast BPR and TQM with cultural appreciation, based on the frameworks outlined in Figures 7.2–7.4.

---

case exercise

By 1987, the then Luton College of Higher Education (LCHE) had reached a stable position in a mature market: change could be accommodated as a gradual, incremental process which proved relatively easy to manage. This all changed with the 1988 Education Reform Act (ERA), which gave rise to LCHE progressing from the status of Institute of Higher Education, able to award some of its own undergraduate and post-graduate degrees under the auspices of the CNAA, to university status, awarding its own undergraduate, taught postgraduate and research degrees. These changes have given rise to a restructuring of manage-ment and faculties, with increased subject specialisation.

Alongside this, the announcement by the UK government of a target to increase higher education student numbers up to the year 2000 (from a then-current ratio of 1 in 5 to a proposed 1 in 3), at a time when the population of 18-year-olds was falling, meant that new courses had to be developed to attract a higher percentage of students in an increasingly competitive market.

To cope with these external forces, a decision was taken (in common with many of the University's competitors) to change from a course-based structure with programmes of study taught throughout the three terms of the academic year, to a modular structure, with students compiling their own programmes of study from modules chosen from anywhere in the University. Under modularity, the teaching year is split into two semesters each of fifteen weeks, with modules being taught

continued . . .

and examined in a single semester. Prior to the 1988 Education Reform Act, LCHE was offering taught courses on the basis of a three-term academic year of thirty-six weeks. Each course was located within a faculty, and was clearly defined in terms of what had to be studied to gain the stated award. Most courses were well established, their management and delivery tried and tested over a number of years. Few were above Higher National Diploma level. The current situation is of a modular scheme of study for predominantly degree courses. The change which this has necessitated may be summarised under four headings:

- The introduction of the modular scheme, under which faculties now offer fields of study within which are a number of modules. In principle, a student can build a study programme by drawing modules from anywhere in the scheme, subject to certain constraints. To control the change to the modular scheme, a decision was taken to use a new management information system (HEMIS), largely replacing tasks which had previously been carried out at departmental level with centralised administration.
- Change to a semester-based year, whereby each module is now studied over fifteen weeks rather than the previous thirty-six, with the attendant alterations to teaching and assessment strategies. Academic staff failed fully to appreciate the effect of reduced time (fifteen weeks against thirty-six) in which to deliver the material. Module content, assessment strategies, rationale and learning outcomes have all had to be rethought to work within the modular framework.
- Increased numbers: the growth over the last four to five years has been from fewer than 3,000 full-time-equivalent students to over 13,000 full-time-equivalent students. It is fair to say that in many areas staff felt overwhelmed by the sheer volume of students. Staff used to running courses with 100 students now, in some cases, were managing fields of over 500, and teaching modules studied by over 1,000.
- The shift of emphasis to almost all degree-level work. Increased research and staff development have been instrumental in the continuous upgrading required to meet the needs of the new curriculum.

How would you recommend that this change be undertaken? Pay particular attention to the structure/culture issues implied by the case.

FURTHER READING

Cao, G., S. A. Clarke and B. Lehaney (1999) 'Towards systemic management of diversity in organisational change', *Journal of Strategic Change* **8**(4): 205–16.

This recent analysis of change management is drawn from an extensive research programme, and summarises the current position regarding the functionalist or planned versus the cultural or incremental debate in change management.

Jackson, M. C. (1987) 'Systems strategies for information management in organisations which are not machines', *International Journal of Information Management* **7**: 187–95.

This paper is the source of Jackson's classification of organisations, and contains further information on the classifications referred to at the beginning of this chapter.

Mintzberg, H. (1991) 'The effective organization: forces and forms', *Sloan Management Review* **32**(2): 54–67.

Though extensively published elsewhere, this is the original source of Mintzberg's classification of organisational forms used in this chapter.

REFERENCES

Adams, J. L. (1987) *Conceptual Blockbusting*, Harmondsworth, Middx: Penguin.

Argyris, C. (1985) *Strategy, Change and Defensive Routines*, New York: Pitman.

Argyris, C. and D. Schon (1974) *Theory in Practice: Increasing Professional Effectiveness*, San Francisco, CA: Jossey-Bass.

Benjamin, R. I. and E. Levinson (1993) 'A framework for managing IT-enabled change', *Sloan Management Review* **34**(4): 23–33.

Boddy, D. and D. Buchanan (1992) *Expertise of the Change Agent*, London: Prentice-Hall.

Cao, G., S. A. Clarke and B. Lehaney (1999) 'Towards systemic management of diversity in organisational change', *Journal of Strategic Change* **8**(4): 205–16.

Carnall, C. A. (1990) *Managing Change in Organisations*, New York: Prentice-Hall.

Fiedler, K. D., V. Grover and J. T. C. Cheng (1994) 'Information technology enabled change: the risks and rewards of business process redesign and automation', *Journal of Information Technology* **9**(4): 267–75.

Hammer, M. and J. Champy (1993) *Reengineering the Corporation: A Manifesto for Business Revolution*, London: Nicholas Brealey.

Jackson, M. C. (1987) 'Systems strategies for information management in organisations which are not machines', *International Journal of Information Management* 7: 187–195.

Jackson, M. C. (1995) 'Beyond the fads: systems thinking for managers', *Systems Research* 12(1): 25–42.

Kudray, L. M. and B. H. Kleiner (1997) 'Global trends in managing change', *Industrial Management* 39(3): 18–20.

McKay, N. F. (1997) 'Radical corporate change: what seems to work – what doesn't?', *Business Forum* 22(1): 8–13.

McSparran, K. and K. Edmunds (1996) 'Changing culture: easier said than done', *Beverage World* 115(1607): 90.

Milliken, F. L. and L. L. Martins (1996) 'Searching for common threads: understanding the multiple effects of diversity in organisational groups', *Academy of Management Review* 21(2): 402–33.

Mintzberg, H. (1987) 'Crafting strategy', *Harvard Business Review* 65(4): 66–75.

Mintzberg, H. (1991) 'The effective organization: forces and forms', *Sloan Management Review* 32(2): 54–67.

Morgan, G. (1986) *Images of Organization*, Beverly Hills, CA: Sage.

Orlikowski, W. J. and J. D. Hofman (1997) 'An improvisational model for change management: the case of groupware technologies', *Sloan Management Review* 38(2): 11–21.

Ryan, H. W. (1992) 'Managing change: the comfort of technology we know', *Information Systems Management* 9(3): 60–2.

Tushman, M. L. and C. A. O'Reilly III (1996) 'Ambidextrous organizations: managing evolutionary and revolutionary change', *California Management Review* 38(4): 8–30.

Part 3

INFORMATION SYSTEMS STRATEGIC MANAGEMENT: LESSONS FOR THE FUTURE

CHAPTER SUMMARY

Key questions

chapter eight **PLANNING AND FORMULATING INFORMATION SYSTEMS STRATEGY**

- How should the domain of information systems be characterised?
- How should the domain of corporate strategy be characterised?
- What do strategic alignment and competitive advantage tell us about ISSM?
- How should ISSM be conceptualised in the light of these findings?

---

chapter nine **THE FUTURE OF INFORMATION SYSTEMS STRATEGIC PLANNING: TECHNICAL OR SOCIAL PROCESS?**

- What does systems thinking have to contribute to the ISSM debate?
- If information systems are seen as social systems, what is to be learnt from social systems theory?
- How does the functionalist/interpretivist/critical systems debate inform ISSM?
- How is the 'framework for information systems strategic management' to be redrawn in the light of these arguments from social theory?

---

chapter
eight

PLANNING AND FORMULATING INFORMATION SYSTEMS STRATEGY

INTRODUCTION

In Chapter one, the concept of information systems as a domain was investigated, emphasising the ideas of the technology versus human-centred debate. In chapter two, the exploration of corporate strategy gave rise to a similar conceptualisation as that reached for IS. Chapters five and six reviewed respectively strategic alignment and competitive advantage from IS. The findings of these chapters are drawn together here to form a basis for an approach to information systems strategic management (ISSM).

In carrying out this analysis, IS is reconceptualised as a predominantly human-centred domain, but one which relies for support on the effective use of technology. The outcome is a new framework for ISSM, at the centre of which lies participant involvement.

LEARNING OBJECTIVES

This chapter will examine:

- the findings of chapters one, two, five and six;

- a reconceptualisation of information systems strategic management based on these findings;

- a strategic action framework drawn from the above reconceptualisation.

INFORMATION SYSTEMS AS A DOMAIN

Chapter one described information systems (IS) as a domain in which the demand from business organisations has traditionally been for 'systems' which show an objective return in terms of cost, efficiency and/or effectiveness, with systems developers being driven to provide low-cost solutions to perceived business problems. The management of IS under this model is governed by a need to design, develop and manage technological solutions to identified problems. In chapter one, however, this approach was challenged and support for an alternative enlisted from studies of systems failure, in which it has been found that up to 90 per cent of information technology (IT) investments do not meet the performance goals set for them

The limitations of technological approaches to IS gave rise, in the 1960s and 1970s, to the so-called 'soft' or human-centred methods, a primary purpose of which is to form a view of the system of concern through the eyes of participants, and to use this to manage the development process. Human-centred methods, it is contended, facilitate participation, help in generating consensus, stimulate creativity, and enlarge the designers' conception of what can be implemented. But the analysis in chapter one goes further, highlighting how recognition of the merits and shortcomings of technological and human-centred approaches to IS gave rise, in the 1970s and beyond, to a number of methods of IS development which may be categorised as mixed; three of the most widely used of these have been ETHICS, multiview, and client-led design.

Human-centred approaches to organisational problem contexts adhere to the interpretive paradigm. Mostly through debate, these methodologies work well in a forum where debate is not constrained, but are unable to secure these conditions where they are not already to be found. In corporate strategy, for example, the organisational context may be one in which the need to collect the views of all involved in the system of concern has been identified (as might be the case in a professional organisation such as a university). However, the debating forum established for this may contain coercive influences (for example, managers who suppress certain viewpoints), or may be composed of members whose abilities in contributing to debate are unequal. Soft methods provide few remedies for these situations.

A further perspective was highlighted in chapter one, in the form of critical theory. Whilst functionalism may be seen as the orthodox approach to systems development, its implicit assumption of one 'reality' which remains the same irrespective of human involvement, and to which systems developers can build 'solutions', has been challenged. Ends are seldom agreed, and the dominant reality is often that of the powerful. Whilst the alternative, interpretivism, does not accept that there is an objective reality but only socially constructed reality, its relativist stance means that systems development outcomes are simply viewed as the result of different, uncritically accepted, socially constructed realities. Critical social theory offers the possibility of moving beyond this debate, to a critically reflective, radical position.

All of this is common to both IS and corporate strategy, in both of which the argument is wrongly cast as the hard–soft debate. So, from the perspective of social theory, current approaches to information systems and corporate strategy may be classified as functionalist or interpretivist. Design approaches to corporate strategy and technology-based approaches to information systems may be seen as functionalist; discovery methods in corporate strategy and human-centred approaches to information systems as interpretivist. Critical social theory therefore offers the potential for combining these approaches with a radical intent. Much work in this area has already been undertaken in the management science domain, and it is this work that is used in the following section to formulate an alternative framework for IS strategy.

IS, it has been argued, can no longer be seen as concerned primarily with the implementation of technological solutions, but emerges, from both practical and theoretical perspectives, as consisting of 'hard' technology-based elements and 'soft' human-centred elements, in an uncomfortable co-existence. Emerging from this is a perceived need to combine both 'hard' and 'soft' approaches, in order to better serve the technical and social aspects of information systems.

CORPORATE STRATEGY: PLANS OR PATTERNS

Chapter two presented the distinction between strategy as a pattern and strategy as a plan as a key issue to be resolved in IS strategic management.

Is it possible, in the IS domain, to write objective strategic plans, agreed on by all concerned and forming the basis of future development? Or are IS strategies just patterns of activity which, whilst evident subsequent to their emergence, cannot be seen in any prior plans of action?

The planning approaches to strategy may be seen as highly design orientated, whereby plans are drawn up which the organisation then uses as a framework for development over the following planning period. This traditional view of strategy as a planning activity, it has been argued, is particularly ill suited to information systems, where both the human-centred nature of the domain, and its reliance on ever-changing technologies, makes planning difficult.

Further, it has been argued, after Mintzberg, that strategy has been almost universally depicted as a deliberate process, whilst the evidence shows this not to be the case, with strategies emerging from the organisation without there having been any deliberate plan. This gives support to the logical incrementalist view, which appears as a way to combine the planning and behavioural approaches to strategy.

A summary of the planning (design) and patterning (discovery) approaches is presented in the box, and demonstrates a hard–soft dichotomy similar to that found in information systems.

Alternative views of corporate srategy

Design	*Discovery*
Plans	Patterns
Planning	Emergent
Design	Debate/disclosure
How	What
Structured	Unstructured
Hard	Soft
Functional	Interpretive
Systematic	Systemic
Reductionist	Holistic

Strategy is divided under two headings: strategy by design and strategy by discovery. Strategy by design encompasses systematic approaches, whereby plans are derived through objective, reductionist methods. Strategy by discovery, by contrast, requires systemic (or holistic – concentrating on the whole as sub-systems in interaction rather than the parts or components in isolation) approaches, favouring participative methods covering the whole system of concern. Contextual issues within the organisation will be at least a partial determinant of the approach taken: a planning method, for example, arguably suiting a mechanistic organisation, incrementalism being more suited to professional adhoc-racies.

As with IS, both views have a place, with a perceived need for a mixture of approaches premised, at least in part, on the organisational context encountered. Furthermore, in respect of corporate strategy as applied to information systems management, strategy by discovery may be seen as long term, concerned with planning for the unknown, or forecasting discontinuities; whilst the design approach may be seen as short term, and concerned with carrying out the IS strategy through the application of information technology. Corporate strategy cannot therefore rely on any one approach, but must craft a combination of strategic methods to fit the organisational form and context.

Planning IS strategy in an 'entrepreneurial adhocratic' organisation

The JayBee* Marketing Agency is highly successful, and has a world-wide reputation for the quality of service it provides across a wide range of industries and products. The agency consists of four directors, each of whom has overall responsibility for an industry sector. Under each of the directors is a marketing team which works on a variety of assignments. Teams find their own work and provide leads to other teams in an ad hoc fashion. The objectives of the agency are very broadly framed and relate to generating an excess of income over expenditure.

During 1999, JayBee attempted to formulate a strategy to guide the organisation over the short to medium term, but found plans impossible to determine in the sort of written, objective format in which it expected to see them.

Following meetings with a consultant, the issue was resolved. JayBee is clearly of an organisational form which does not lend itself to the 'design' approach to strategic planning, and instead decided to form looser ideas through participative sessions with all staff.

Early signs are that all in the organisation are becoming involved in this increased strategic focus. Operational (day-to-day almost) commitment and return has never been a problem at JayBee, but now this is being seen in a much longer-term framework in which is identified the patterns of expected future activity.

* JayBee is a pseudonym.

Taking into account the above positions on IS and corporate strategy, a clear problem emerges in relation to information systems: what is required in IS strategic management is not the forecasting of some repetitive pattern or predictable event, but the 'discontinuities', of which the technological developments which so often enable information systems are a prime example. The answer is not to attempt to forecast such discontinuities, since such forecasting is clearly impossible, but to react once they are identified. Strategy under this approach becomes 'planning' for the unknown, and as such must make use of subjective judgement.

STRATEGIC ALIGNMENT

Chapter five proposed a strategic model (Figure 5.1) in which all the elements of corporate and information systems strategy are aligned, so that an organisation's information resource is placed to support that organisation's strategic and, ultimately, operational activity.

The alignment 'problem' in the domain of information strategy has frequently been wrongly cast as a need to align *information technology* with corporate strategy. Recent evidence points to the corporate, business and information domains all requiring to be continuously aligned within information needs analysis, and that information systems and information technology should be seen as supporting or supplying that need.

Alignment of IT, IS, information and corporate strategies, the framework for which is encapsulated in Figure 5.1, then becomes a continuous process of aligning the business domain (business strategy and business organisation) with the IS domain (IS infrastructure and processes and IS strategy) in accordance with corporate strategy and the organisation's IS map. This approach to alignment requires that the alignment perspective relevant to the organisation must be determined, and that only then is the organisation ready to move on to implementing strategic alignment.

Aligning IT with corporate strategy: 'the wrong way to do it!'

It is 1996, and Millennium Electronics is engaged in the manufacture and sale of peripheral components for the computer industry. Their corporate strategic plan is well formed, and in effect tracks the product development necessary to support its main customers, who are microcomputer manufacturers. Strategy is pretty simple: 'If such and such a manufacturer sees the next

continued . . .

generation of processors as so many hundred MHz, we make sure
we have the right components in production to support these power
levels.' Since all this is so clear, the IT strategy is equally simple:
to provide the necessary IT support which will enable the corporate
strategy to work.

By mid-1998, Millennium Electronics was in receivership, having
failed to keep pace with the rapidly changing world of computer
technology.

Maybe strategy was not the cause of this: perhaps other more
fundamental things went wrong. Nevertheless it seems the 'strategy
execution' perspective taken was entirely at odds with the type of
organisation. A technology potential or competitive potential
perspective would seem much more in keeping and, if applied
properly, could have offered some real strategic advantages to the
organisation.

Information needs must then be related to the internal and external
business and information systems domains of the organisation. For
information systems and information technology analysis, the strategic
grid (Figure 5.8) and the technology implementation grid (Figure 5.10)
have been identified as valuable analysis tools. The means of undertaking
this process is seen to depend on participative study, based on soft methods
and the findings from action research.

COMPETITIVE ADVANTAGE

It seems clear that, through the twenty years leading to the new millennium, the focus for competitive advantage has moved away from IT and
towards IS, highlighting the use made of the technology within a given
organisation rather than just the technology itself. It appears that both
IT and IS need to be integrated into an organisation, and that it is the
organisational system which should be the focus of attention.

The greatest promise of sustainability comes from human interaction.
In terms of its information resource, an organisation clearly stands to gain
from the strategic use of *information*. Focus on IT alone, or even on IS,
seems unhelpful: the real competitive advantage comes from the *use* of
technology and systems. There is clear evidence from empirical studies
that, even where a number of major players within an industry have access
to the same technology, some succeed by using that technology better,
while others fail. Sustainability comes from the interaction of interdependent sub-systems within a system of human activity: this kind of

competitive advantage is not 'planned for' in any instrumental sense, but is the natural outcome of information which is strategically managed.

A RECONCEPTUALISATION: INFORMATION SYSTEMS STRATEGIC MANAGEMENT (ISSM)

Analysis of chapters one, two, five and six points to a reconceptualisation of IS strategic management as a human-centred domain, and the findings from these chapters can now be summarised to provide a new approach to information systems strategic management (ISSM). The basis for this new approach is summarised below, and the process presented in Figure 8.1.

In summary, information systems strategic management may be seen to depend on:

- an approach to information systems which recognises the value of both human-centred and technology-based issues. The likelihood is that, within a given organisational context, a mix of approaches will be required, though the overwhelming perception of IS as fundamentally a social domain determines that any approach to ISSM should focus on the participants within the problem context;
- an approach to corporate strategy which is primarily subjective: strategy is the domain of those involved in and affected by the problem situation, not something that can be objectively planned and worked towards in a scientific, deterministic manner;
- an alignment perspective, at the heart of the ISSM process, which is driven by information needs, as determined by those involved in the system of concern. We are not seeking to write a corporate strategic plan and then 'align' IS, or even worse IT, with it, but to develop IS and corporate strategy in tandem, through an alignment perspective relevant to the nature of the organisation concerned;
- a view of sustainable competitive advantage which sees it not as emanating from the application of technology *per se*, but recognises that competitive advantage can be secured by organisations even where they use the same technologies. The sustainability of advantage from information comes from how that information is used, and is therefore a human issue rather than a technological one.

All the evidence of ISSM, therefore, points to participant involvement at the heart of the process. Figure 8.1 presents a process which recognises this.

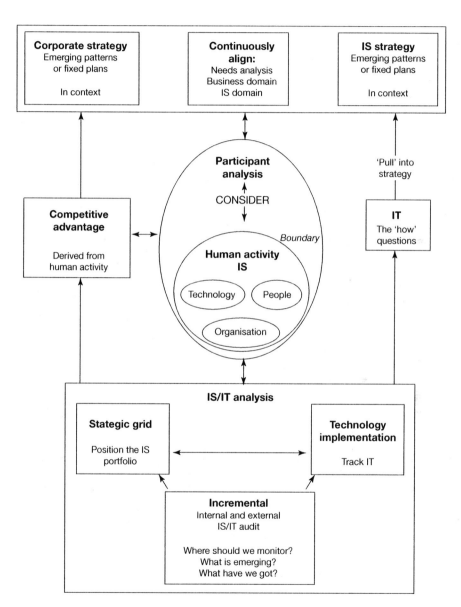

Figure 8.1 **A framework for information systems strategic management**

Figure 8.1 presents the core of ISSM as analysis of the system of concern by participants: those involved in and affected by the system. First, a holistic view of the system must be formed. This, represented by the Participant circle at the centre of the figure, will be a human activity system, but will almost certainly include organisational and technological sub-systems. The importance of this part of the analysis cannot be overstated: IS strategic management is not something to be conducted by a privileged group of experts or managers; the necessary knowledge on which an organisation must build is held by the members of that organisation, all of whom must be represented in the strategy process. A number of methodologies or techniques are available to assist with this process, including a wide range of soft methods (see Clarke *et al.*, 1998 for a summary). The approach I have found to be most helpful involves the use of total systems intervention (see chapter three), although work on critically informed intervention is moving forward rapidly, and the reader more directly interested in these issues would be well advised to appraise him/herself of future developments.

The rest of the analysis must be carried out with participants at the centre of the activity. This is shown in Figure 8.1 as a number of inter-dependent strands to be considered in managing the information systems strategy process. First, the present position in relation to corporate and IS strategy must be determined (see Figures 5.8 and 5.10). The form this takes will depend on the context of the system (for example, mechanistic, adhocratic, and so on: Mintzberg, 1991), but in most organisations is likely to be a matter of determining patterns of activity, past and emerging, rather than looking at some plan which purports to be the organisation's strategy. The ISSM process proper then commences with an information needs analysis (Figure 5.1), from which the corporate and IS strategies can be developed interdependently, stressing either the business or the IS domain, depending on the 'planning perspective' taken. Focus on information needs throughout the ISSM process enables alignment of corporate and IS strategies to be continuously monitored, and followed according to the relevant alignment perspective. Information needs analysis combined with continuous strategic alignment is the primary process which drives ISSM.

Simultaneously with this primary activity, there also needs to be ongoing participant analysis of the organisation's competitive position, its strategic use of information systems, and the availability and implementation of IT solutions. Many participant groups within an organisation have knowledge of and a view on its competitive position, and all should be drawn into the discussion of 'competitive advantage'. Similarly, there will be identifiable groups who can contribute to the IS/IT analysis. The use of Porter and

Millar's 'information intensity matrix' and Porter's 'five forces model' (see chapter six) could be employed here. These activities feed the strategic study, the IS/IT analysis doing so partly through competitive positioning of the IS portfolio, and partly by strategy 'pulling in' IT solutions.

CONCLUSIONS

The argument in this chapter has been for corporate, IS and IT strategy to be developed within a common framework, based on participant analysis.

All of the evidence drawn from IS, corporate strategy and the strategic domains of IS, such as competitive advantage and strategic alignment, points to participant analysis being at the centre of both the corporate and IS strategy domains. This is complicated, however, by the need to utilise technology to support the strategy process, which requires technology-based and human-centred analysis to be used together within ISSM.

The solution is presented as a strategic ISS process to be followed (Figure 8.1). Two key factors drive the process and must be identified:

1 What is the system of concern?
2 Who are the participants to be involved in the analysis?

Strategic issues of corporate/IS strategic alignment, competitive advantage, and IS and IT analysis are then all considered through the participants' view of the system of concern.

This brings the study of ISSM almost to a close. However, there are still some unresolved issues from, primarily, the theoretical study in chapter three. Primary among these issues are the conceptualisation of the system and the nature of participant involvement. These will now be considered in the final chapter, and will be seen to indicate a modification of the 'framework for ISSM' for the future.

SUMMARY

- Information systems should be seen as a human-centred domain, enabled by technology, and therefore requiring a mixture of human-centred and technology-based methods.
- Corporate strategy is similarly and predominantly a human-centred domain, in which planning/design issues should not be allowed to dominate.
- Information systems strategic issues further support the domain as being human-centred.

- The overall conclusion is that ISSM needs to be approached from a perspective informed by participative analysis, and a framework has been presented to achieve this.

REVIEW QUESTIONS

1 What are the key factors in ISSM, corporate strategy, strategic alignment and competitive advantage from IS which might be said to determine both domains as human-centred?

2 What are the differences between viewing a system of concern in a reductionist way and viewing the same system holistically? How might each of these views affect your approach to ISSM?

3 Describe the process of ISSM using the framework presented in Figure 8.1 as a basis.

DISCUSSION QUESTIONS

1 In a mechanistic organisation, corporate strategy can be planned with reasonable certainty. IS strategic management therefore becomes simply a matter of designing the information systems to support the corporate strategy. Do you agree?

2 ISSM is impossible without the willing involvement of all involved in and affected by the organisational problem context. Discuss.

---

case exercise

Case 1

A-Plan Manufacturing have called you in as a consultant to advise on the provision of electronic mail between all staff, and has asked you to help prepare a strategic brief to achieve this.

A-Plan sees the problem as predominantly operational and technical – they need a computer network and an email system. You are not so convinced, as your previous experience has led you to understand that many computer networks are underused and that, particularly in organisations where staff are not highly computer literate, use of them is actively avoided.

continued . . .

The 'solution', in your opinion, is an approach which takes more account of the staff involved and affected by the proposed system than just the technology. You have managed to talk the managers of the company round to trying your approach, but how would you now proceed?

Case 2

One of the new universities wishes to boost its research activity, and it has been suggested that an academic network, both internal and externally linked, would be of immense value to those involved. Your immediate concerns centre on the idea of what constitutes an 'academic network', especially as you have a strong feeling that the main decision-makers see this in technical terms. Pursuing the idea of a 'network of people in communication', how would you proceed to conduct a strategy feasibility study?

FURTHER READING

Clarke, S. A. and B. Lehaney (1997) 'Information systems strategic planning: a model for implementation in changing organisations', *Systems Research and Behavioral Science* **14**(2): 129–36.
This paper presents some preliminary work on the formulation of the 'framework for information systems strategic management', and offers further support and references which may be of interest to readers.

Mintzberg, H., J. B. Quinn and S. Ghoshal (1998) *The Strategy Process*, rev. European edn, Hemel Hempstead, Herts.: Prentice-Hall.
This is a collection of edited chapters and covers, in summary, all the corporate strategic background to this chapter. An excellent starting point from which to undertake a study of approaches to strategic thinking.

Porter, M. E. (1990) *The Competitive Advantage of Nations*, London: Macmillan.
Porter is the definitive author on competitive advantage. More detail on many of the models and ideas used in this chapter are to be found in this text.

REFERENCES

Baets, W. (1992) 'Aligning information systems with business strategy', *Journal of Strategic Information Systems* **1**(4): 205–13.

Clarke, S. A., B. Lehaney and S. Martin (1998) 'A theoretical framework for facilitating methodological choice', *Systemic Practice and Action Research* **11**(3): 295–318.

Venkatraman, N., J. C. Henderson and S. Oldach (1993) 'Continuous strategic alignment: exploiting information technology capabilities for competitive success', *European Management Journal* **11**(2): 139–49.

chapter
nine

THE FUTURE OF INFORMATION SYSTEMS STRATEGIC MANAGEMENT: A TECHNICAL OR SOCIAL PROCESS?

INTRODUCTION

Chapter eight built on the findings of chapters one, two, five and six to develop a framework for information systems strategic management (ISSM) based on a reconceptualisation of IS and corporate strategy as human-centred domains. The objective of this chapter is to conclude the text from a theoretical perspective, developing the ideas in chapter three in the light of the discussions throughout the rest of the book.

Since the theme throughout has been IS from a human-centred perspective, this chapter begins with a view of IS as social systems. First, what are systems, and why should they be important to the study of ISSM? This leads into a discussion of systems thinking, and the special characteristics of social systems, in particular the type of social system that might be most relevant to ISSM.

Drawing more deeply on the analysis of chapter three, and the 'framework for information systems strategic management' in chapter eight (Figure 8.1), a foundation for ISSM is sought which is informed by critical social theory. The Habermasian position is discussed and critiqued, leaving the necessary underpinning to ISSM, whilst located in critical social theory, more generally dependent on Kantian thought, as applied within Western capitalist economies.

Finally, the chapter concludes with a revised 'critical' framework for ISSM.

LEARNING OBJECTIVES

This chapter will examine:

- systems thinking, and its relevance to ISSM;

- information systems strategic management from a social systems perspective;

- a critical systems approach to ISSM;

- a critique of Habermas as a basis for ISSM, and a return to Kantian thinking;

- a revised critical systems framework for the process of information systems strategic management.

INFORMATION SYSTEMS AS SOCIAL SYSTEMS

Systems

The argument of this section is that systems thinking has a direct application within the study of IS generally, and information systems strategic management (ISSM) in particular. A technological approach to IS reduces the complexity of the system of study and attempts to define it in terms of rules and procedures by which given inputs can be turned into predictable outputs: a so-called deterministic system. A human-centred approach is quite different. Human activity systems are 'complex' and 'adaptive' and cannot be fully described in terms of rules and procedures. Deterministic systems can be addressed through scientific method. The fundamental basis of science, reductionism, can be used to reduce a system to component parts, devise laws for these components and find the laws hold true when studying the system as a whole. As complexity increases, however, such an approach can be seen to fail.

Systems thinking

The properties of systems may be summarised as:

- Boundary

  All systems must have a boundary, determining the system's scope, and separating it from other systems.

- Emergence

  Any system has properties which emerge only when all the sub-systems of which it is comprised are inter-acting.

- Holism

  Sub-systems or components cannot be viewed independently: the system must always be seen as a whole.

- Interdependence

  Sub-systems within the system are interdependent: changes in one sub-system will affect others.

- Hierarchy

  Systems will normally contain a number of other systems or sub-systems, which will be identifiable as a hierarchy. Investigation at one level cannot replace investigation at another.

- Transformation

  All systems have a transformation process: manufacturing systems, for example, produce something.

- Communication and Control

  Systems require communication and control mechanisms.

The problem of organisational systems rests on whether they are viewed as designed physical or human activity systems. A 'designed' perspective assumes a mechanical or technological view, whereas, by contrast, human activity systems cannot make such rule-based assumptions. In this respect, the systems problem parallels the technology/human-centred problem in IS and strategy.

Consider a computerised information system. Whilst it may be possible to 'engineer' the computer sub-system, this is not possible with an information system consisting of human activity. Figure 9.1 is taken from a study of the student record information system at the University of Luton. The 'existing record system' could have been replaced, arguably by involving only the system designers. However, even at an operational level, the wider needs of government, management and users were seen to be important to this analysis. In determining the *strategy* for this information system such a holistic view proved essential. System boundaries were determined (in participative forums), and the system seen as a non-deterministic, open system with (possibly as yet unrecognised) emergent properties.

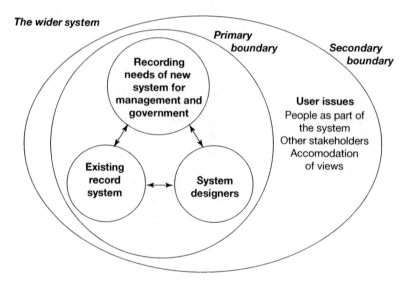

Figure 9.1 **An information system: a technical or human activity system?**

Source: Clarke and Lehaney (2000)

Designed systems and human activity systems

Designed systems are produced by humankind to fulfil a particular purpose. Whilst they are associated with human activity systems, the primary focus on design determines the approach to such systems in ISSM as technology-based.

Human activity systems contain human beings with 'novel' characteristics, the most important of which is self-consciousness. So, as we have freedom of choice, whilst the outcome of a human activity system may be *predicted*, that outcome can never be assumed to have been *inevitable*. This makes human activity systems logically quite different from designed systems: scientific principles may be applied to the latter, but for the former it is argued we must start with an account of the observer and the point of view from which the observations were made.

SOCIAL SYSTEMS

Social systems may be classified as complex adaptive systems, being seen by many as the most adaptive of all systems. Technology-based analysis introduces systematic rationality into human decision-making, where the problem is to select, among a number of alternatives, an efficient means of achieving an end we know we wish to reach. In IS, what technology-based methods have been very good at achieving is the provision of computer systems that mechanise existing, less-efficient systems of information transmission and/or data capture, and provide it in a more timely and cost efficient way. So, just as the engineer who knows what is needed is a bridge to connect one side of a river to another can systematically approach the goal of building the bridge, so the same is true where the goal is to take a known situation and provide a computer-based solution to a known problem.

A computerised credit control system

In the mid-1970s, the UK subsidiary of a US dental products manufacturing company held the franchise for selling all the company's products throughout the UK. The operation was small in terms of personnel, with only twelve full-time employees, but credit control involved the collection of over £500,000 per month – a significant sum at the time.

continued . . .

Invoices were manually prepared, as were all the organisation's accounting records. The credit controller had the task of scanning and updating these records on a daily basis to satisfy the credit requirements of the parent company.

In 1977, a computer system was installed to record the information from invoices and aid the credit controller in her task of trying to keep down customer debts to an average of 45 days.

The system was simple to specify and install. It was a deterministic, 'transaction processing' system: once the invoice inputs and customer characteristics were in the system, collection of debts largely proceeded according to set rules which seldom needed to be broken. Within three months of installation, credit had been reduced by seven days, representing an extra £100,000 plus in the bank; in addition the credit controller was finding the task much easier to perform and was giving time to other activities in the accounts department.

The moral of this *true* story is that technology-based methods are fine when applied to the right problem context.

Within information systems, the categorisation of social theories undertaken by Burrell and Morgan (1979) has been used to inform the domain. In chapter three, Burrell and Morgan's positioning of all social theories into one of four paradigms (functionalist, interpretivist, radical humanist and radical structuralist) was introduced. Figure 3.1 (p. 45) shows this categorisation, together with a positioning of information systems methodologies and corporate planning perspectives (Clarke and Lehaney, 1999).

The subjective/objective dimension of this classification has been discussed at length in chapters one and two, and is reproduced in the technology-based versus human-centred positions in IS and the design versus discovery debate in strategic management. Our concern in this chapter is with the regulation/radical change dimension. All IS methodologies (Figure 3.1) are cast as regulative: that is, from the social theory perspective, they do not have the power to change the status quo within an organisation or problem context. To overcome this, a number of authors in management generally, and IS specifically, have recommended that support be sought from the radical humanist paradigm.

Radical humanism is represented in management studies through critical social theory, and chapter three showed how the work of Habermas (1971) has been taken to provide the primary theoretical support to underpin this work. For a summary of the Habermasian position see pp. 52–3.

Regulatory methods in a 'radical' problem context

The Dean of Business at a US university saw the future of the faculty resting on a major reorganisation, rationalising the current seven departments into four. Whilst there were substantial management gains to be realised, both in terms of cost and the increased efficiency of larger departments with fewer chains of command, staff were likely to be resistant to the idea.

To air the issues, a summary of the proposed reorganisation was distributed, and participative sessions with each of the seven departments were set up. The sessions went well, with genuine issues being aired and a number of points raised which appeared to need more clarification before proceeding.

The next stage of the process was interesting. A summary of the proceedings was circulated from the Dean's office, effectively giving the green light to the reorganisation, and citing the participative sessions as part of the approval mechanism: no mention was made of any changes to the plan as laid out in the Dean's original summary document.

The reorganisation went ahead, and academic staff largely continued to go about their daily business as before, viewing the whole process with suspicion, and seeing less purpose in involvement in any future such initiatives. What had happened was that participation had apparently been encouraged, but in the end power had been exercised to force a solution: the changes had been carried out in support of the status quo.

CRITICAL SYSTEMS

A critical systems approach to ISSM, by recognising the merits of both hard (technology-based) and soft (human-centred) methods, offers a way forward from the current emphasis on, at worst, solely technological issues and, at best, a technological approach which has added to it some acceptance of the need to deal with human activity. To date, within management studies and IS, the primary theoretical support for this approach has been grounded in the work of Habermas, in particular his theory of knowledge constitutive interests (Habermas, 1971: Table 3.3).

Habermasian theory as a basis for information systems: a critique

The critical stream in information systems has, since its commencement in the early 1980s, relied almost entirely on Habermas's theory of knowledge constitutive interests (KCI) for its theoretical underpinning. There is, however, a wealth of critical theory available to the interventionist, emanating from the foundations laid by Kant (1724–1804). Kant's exposure of 'synthetic *a priori* statements' brings forward the idea that we all carry around with us certain 'mental baggage', which we accept uncritically. In Western capitalist countries this appears, for example, in the almost unquestioning acceptance on the part of many that capitalism is right and no other alternative can be better. But Kant is saying more than just this: not only do we accept this uncritically, but it becomes so ingrained in our culture that we no longer even think about it. This insight shows how an uncritical approach may lead to a false consciousness (for example, we falsely believe we are making objective decisions, when in fact they are conditioned by an embedded understanding that we no longer challenge): a critical approach, it is argued, is able to expose this. More recently this has been explored (see, for example, Midgley, 1995; Brocklesby and Cummings, 1996; Probert, 1996). Brocklesby and Cummings (1996) refer to a historical development through Hegel to Marx and thereby to the Frankfurt School, the main contributors to which they identify as Horkheimer, Adorno and Marcuse. Probert (1996) queries the exclusion of Benjamin and gives more weight to the work of Adorno.

The first criticism of using Habermas's knowledge constitutive interests (KCI) as the basis for critical systems thinking is that it is simply temporally convenient. There is no reason to ignore all other theorists in favour of Habermas, and doing so leaves critical systems (CS) with a limited theoretical justification. Even if the theoretical underpinning for CS is limited to current, or most recent, influential critical thinkers, the work of Foucault, at least, cannot be ignored. For example, Habermas has concentrated on a view of emancipation in which methods can be developed to emancipate people as a whole, which in management studies has been applied to the emancipation of groups, or emancipation within organisational interventions. Foucault, by contrast, sees emancipation as an essentially individual concept, and aims to give participants the tools by which to liberate themselves. In Foucauldian terms, emancipation of participants within an interventionist situation is simply not possible.

Even if it were accepted as justifiable to cast Habermas as currently the most significant critical thinker, the choice of his knowledge constitution theory as a basis for the development of a critical approach to organisation studies can be questioned. Midgley (1995), for example, argues that the theory of knowledge constitutive interests supports a predict and control approach, thereby perpetuating a view of the human domination of nature which, it could be argued, will have detrimental consequences. Midgley proposes a solution based on Habermas's work on universal pragmatics, in which Habermas argues that communication aimed at reaching an understanding always involves the raising of four validity claims, which may be categorised as comprehensibility, truth, rightness and sincerity. Midgley (1995) has undertaken some initial work to develop these as an alternative basis for a pluralist theory. Truth is seen by Midgley as relating to the objective/external world, and thereby to hard, cybernetic methods; rightness to the normative, social world, and hence soft methods; and sincerity to the subjective, internal world, and cognitive methods such as cognitive mapping and personal construct theory (see Kelly, 1955; Eden, 1988, 1994). Similarly Oliga (1996) and Foong *et al.* (1997) have focused on Habermas's (1987) system–lifeworld concept, which conceptualises 'society as a whole' as consisting of lifeworld: the inner needs of its members addressed via communicative action; and system: the outer needs addressed by material reproduction through labour. The outer needs are concerned with 'system integration' and the inner needs with 'social integration', and only if balanced, argues Habermas (1987: 152), does society as a whole become '*systematically stabilised* complexes of action of *socially integrated* groups'. In modernity, it is argued, system dominates, with the lifeworld undermined by 'transfers of communicative infra-structures to the system' (Foong *et al.*, 1997).

Recent work by Hirschheim, Klein and Newman (1991) looks at the application of social action theories from Weber, Etzioni and Habermas (Weber, 1947; Etzioni, 1967; Habermas, 1971, 1976) as a basis for a theory of information systems development formed from seven elements: consensus, resistance, conflict, knowledge, subjective meanings, power and human interests. Knowledge and power seem central to the approach, though the work lacks advice as to practical action.

The picture that therefore emerges is of a critical approach to IS which is underpinned explicitly by critical social theory, but which gives insufficient consideration to the range of critical social theories available. The adoption of an alternative (for example, Foulcauldian) perspective is seen seriously to undermine the emancipatory commitment, and thereby the whole interventionist framework.

A CRITICAL APPROACH TO INFORMATION
SYSTEMS: BEYOND HABERMAS

To underpin this section, a solution is sought from the roots of critical theory which, from a modernist perspective, may be seen to lie in Kantian (1724–1804) thought. From this position, no longer are we to be concerned simply with the system that exists: 'what *is*'; we need to be considering the normative position: 'what *ought to be*'.

Kant's three basic questions in the search for knowledge are:

- *What can I know?* representing an 'interest in *mapping social reality*'. Pursuing this with critical intent means understanding the totality of the system in comparison to the representation of it, which is our map. The maps reflect our *a priori* conditions, and the totality can be surfaced by an approach to boundary critique (Ulrich, 1983: 260).
- *What ought I to do?* governed by the principle 'design for improvement of the human condition, and reflect on the inevitable *lack* of moral perfection in your designs, *as if* those affected by your designs were self responsible moral beings' (ibid.: 261).
- *What may I hope?* Since, according to Ulrich, there is no guarantee of improvement through planning, such guarantee must be sought, albeit imperfectly, through broad involvement of the involved and affected, consultation and consensus building.

Ulrich's (1983) work has focused on these issues, and uses critique in three distinct ways:

1 to surface the normative content of systems designs;
2 applied to boundary judgements in helping determine the system of concern;
3 to reveal the normative content in 'system' – to challenge 'objectivist delusion':

The key problem that makes applied science, as compared with basic science, so difficult to justify lies in the *normative content* that its propositions gain in the context of application (Ulrich, 1991).

Ulrich's approach is based on a partial reconstruction of Kantian thinking and argues for a return to the Aristotelian position, which distinguished theory and practice, and which he sees to have been lost in the Enlightenment, with the coming to pre-eminence of instrumental reason at the expense of practical reason. Kant saw this as a distinction between theoretical reason, applied instrumentally to determine truth claims, and practical reason, concerned with the normative validity of practical propositions. In the former, 'formal-logical reasoning proceeds in a linear and unreflective manner', whilst in the latter, 'dialectical reasoning breaks through the given premises, and frees us to overcome our fixed patterns of thinking – and our being contented with them' (Ulrich, 1983: 268). Ulrich further argues reason to be 'theoretical if it secures critical understanding of *what is*; [and] practical if it secures critical understanding of *what ought to be*' (ibid.: 220). From this perspective, rational planning no longer takes the position of instrumental decision-making according to a certain set of norms: 'planning is rational, from the perspective of this study, if the involved planners and the affected citizens make transparent to themselves and to each other this normative content' (ibid.: 20).

A 'critical' view of 'rational' planning

Consider an organisation that wished to lay out its future plans for IT support of its distribution operation. What does a 'rational' approach to this imply?

Rational = Instrumental

The organisation commissions a study of existing systems and the needs of the new distribution system. This is specified by systems analysts, and a computer-based system designed, developed and implemented.

Rational = 'Normative'

Any existing administrative and computer-based 'systems' are ignored. All involved in the system of concern are drawn into a discussion of what the new system ought to be, where the system consists of all issues within the boundary as determined by those participants.

Many of you will think this sounds rather convoluted. All I can say is: try it – it works!

But critique is not merely against a set of norms; it requires a critique of the norms themselves. In this latter form, critique can be said to be self-reflective rather than instrumental, or 'practical' in Kantian terminology, and involves bringing into view the values or norms that underlie the position taken or judgements made. Such critique and reflection requires a dialectic. In the process of planning, the purpose of the dialectic (Ulrich, 1983: 289) is to bring together all participants in the planning process through a discourse which surfaces their normative positions. This leads Ulrich (1991) to see 'justification' in the applied sciences as concerning both the involved and the affected, and requiring a grounding not in rational scientific logic but in a model of rational discourse.

To intervene within a problem context requires that the scope of that context be defined. In systems terms this requires determining the boundary of the system, but frequently this is done in an arbitrary and uncritical way. Ulrich (1991) makes a distinction between not just that which is controllable and that which is uncontrollable, but also the unknown or even unknowable, and advances the view that boundaries are most frequently drawn to include the controllable. In response to this he calls for a 'critically normative understanding of boundary judgements . . . Systems thinking that is not *critically normative* in this sense will evade all significant problems of practical reason and thereby fail to be either practical or scientific' (Ulrich, 1983: 25).

A further theme inherent in Ulrich's (1988) work is that of emancipation to combat coercive influences. Here he draws on Habermas (1971: 240), who asserts that, in both theoretical and practical reason, decisions are reached by 'the peculiarly unforced force of the better argument' rather than by resort to power or deception. Ulrich (1983: 221) also refers to Kant's moral idea whereby he takes practical to mean that which is possible through freedom. Hence the introduction of emancipation to the debate: 'By "the practical", I mean everything that is possible through freedom' (Kant, [1787] 1929: 828).

These themes from Kantian thought can now be applied to provide a critical systems approach to ISSM.

ISSM AS CRITICAL SYSTEMS PRACTICE

Though theoretically complex, the *practice* of applying critique within ISSM is relatively straightforward, and can be seen from a reinterpretation of the 'framework for information systems strategic management' (Figure 8.1). This reinterpretation gives us a revised *critical* process for ISSM, represented by Figure 9.2. From the theoretical argument of this chapter, the revised critical framework for ISSM can now be developed (Figure 9.2). The basic issues to be included in the framework are described below:

- Critique within the ISSM process should have the explicit aim of exposing the 'normative' content of the system 'design'. In other words, it should not just focus on 'what is', but should aim to show what 'ought to be'. The aim is, through dialectical reasoning, to overcome fixed patterns of thinking.

- Similarly, critique should address the values and norms of the system. These values will underlie the position taken and may seriously undermine realistic analysis of the system. How often, for example, are we expected to see organisational problems in a framework of profit maximisation? But even company directors know that there is much more driving the company than just profit: failure to explicitly recognise these 'true' values leaves planning with an unrealistic foundation.
- The justification for this approach lies in the ability to claim that it is based on rational discourse. Such a claim is seen to fail if all involved and affected in the system of concern are not included as participants.
- Boundaries must be set *critically*. Too often the system boundary is drawn around that which is seen to be 'controllable', but this is an inadequate perspective. Commonly in IS the complaint is raised that users cannot be involved in decision-making because they do not understand what they want, or even what is possible. Critical systems meets this problem head on: the system boundary must include the unknown or even *unknowable*.

Including these issues gives rise to the revised framework presented in Figure 9.2.

The application of the framework outlined in the figure is described in detail in chapter eight. The additional issue included here, which now completes the framework, is the recommendation to undertake participant analysis:

1 through the inclusion of all those involved in and affected by the system of concern;
2 through a critical process, applying Kantian critique. A key issue here in IS, and an excellent starting point for IS analysis, is boundary setting, which must not be uncritically determined, but must be approached through participant-informed, critical analysis;
3 applying critique within the ISSM process, with the explicit aim of: exposing the 'normative' content of the system 'design' (what 'ought to be'); aiming to overcome fixed patterns of thinking through dialectical reasoning; addressing the values and norms of the system.

A number of approaches are available to help with this process, key among which is the work of Midgley and Ulrich (see references below).

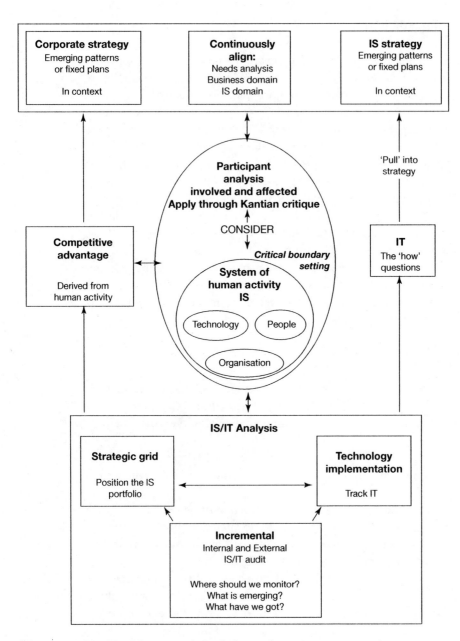

Figure 9.2 **A critical framework for information systems strategic management**

CONCLUSIONS

So what does this mean for ISSM? Critical theory and systems thinking address the participative issues in ISSM and question whether participation is 'real'. The outcome is a series of modifications to the 'framework for information systems strategic management' which are described below.

The focus of these modifications is the 'participant analysis', at the centre of Figure 9.2, through which the system of concern is addressed. First, system boundaries must be *critically* determined. The system must not stop at that which is 'controllable', but must include all sub-systems seen to be important by participants. Typically this will mean extending beyond the technical, computer-based sub-system, to include all relevant organisational and human activity systems. The system of concern will never be fixed, but will be subject to change as the investigation progresses.

Once the system is (preliminarily) determined, participant analysis is recommended to include all those involved in and affected by the system. This is a significant demand, and whilst it is not possible to be prescriptive as to how this should be achieved, the primary consideration is that it should be an ongoing requirement, open to consideration and modification by participants. Further, this participant analysis is to be applied as Kantian critique. What is of interest is not some notional extant system or some objective statement of what the system consists of, but a view principally derived from participant involvement of what the system *ought to be*.

SUMMARY

- The properties of systems can be seen to make systems study directly relevant to ISSM.
- Information systems should be viewed as human activity systems, and investigated theoretically through social theory.
- A study of social systems reveals IS and corporate strategy to be domains dominated by regulative methods.
- A radical humanist approach, grounded in Kantian thinking, offers a way forward from this dilemma.
- The application of critical thinking to ISSM has led to a reconceptualisation of the ISSM process.

REVIEW QUESTIONS

1 What are the properties of systems? Why are they important in ISSM?

2 What are Burrell and Morgan's four paradigms? Why is the radical humanist paradigm seen to be relevant to ISSM?

3 In undertaking 'rational' planning, what is the meaning of 'critical'?

DISCUSSION QUESTIONS

1 Consider an information system with which you have been involved. How would you conceptualise this in systems terms? What effect would this conceptualisation have on the operational and strategic development of the system?

2 What is the critical perspective we are trying to arrive at for ISSM? How does this differ from a view based on Habermas's theory of knowledge constitutive interests?

3 The thrust of this chapter is towards *critically rational* strategic management of information systems. What is meant by *critically rational*?

---

case exercise

Critical thinking:

- requires a dialectic – it must be participative;
- must aim to expose the normative content – what 'ought to be';
- must apply critique to content and 'material conditions';
- requires critical determination of the system boundary.

One technique developed to deal with this is the 'critical boundary questions' of Ulrich, part of his critical systems heuristics methodology.

The analysis below uses Ulrich's critical boundary questions to investigate the proposed implementation of a computer systems email network in a major UK university. The answers on the left were taken from discussions with those involved in and affected by the system. Your task is to answer the questions on the right from your own perspective.

How do your answers differ, and what is the significance, in your view, of this difference?

Critical boundary questions

Question	'Is' mode	'Ought' mode
1	Who is the client? Whose purposes are served by the system? Management, academics and administrative staff	Who ought to be the client?
2	What is the purpose? To enable email between all staff	What ought to be the purpose?
3	What is the measure of success? All staff connected to the system	What ought to be the measure?
4	Who is the decision taker? University directorate	Who ought to be the decision taker?
5	What conditions are actually controlled by the decision taker? Initial decision and expenditure	What components of the system ought to be controlled by the decision taker?
6	What conditions are not controlled by the decision taker? Operational decisions	What resources and conditions ought to be part of the system's environment?
7	Who is the system's designer? University computer services	Who ought to be the system's designer?
8	Who is involved as an expert, what is the nature of the expertise, and what role does the expert play? University networking, plus suppliers	What kind of expertise ought to be involved, who should exercise it, and what should his/her role be?
9	Where is the guarantee of success? With experts, political support, etc.? With experts	Where ought the guarantee of success be?
10	Who represents the concerns of the affected (but not involved)? Users, but poorly represented	Who ought to represent these concerns? Who among the affected ought to become involved?
11	Are the affected given the opportunity to emancipate themselves? No	To what extent ought the affected be given such an opportunity?
12	What world view underlies the system of concern? Western capitalist economy	On what world view ought the design of the system be based?

FURTHER READING

Burrell, G. and G. Morgan (1979) *Sociological Paradigms and Organisational Analysis*, London: Heinemann.
Anyone wishing to understand in outline the application of social theory to organisational studies must start with this text. All the paradigmatic issues are discussed here in depth, but in a way that does not obscure understanding.

Ulrich, W. (1983) *Critical Heuristics of Social Planning: A New Approach to Practical Philosophy*, Berne: Haupt.
Ulrich's primary text introduces the methodology of critical systems heuristics, within a wider framework of critical social theory, grounded in Kantian thinking. The exposition of critical theory, and its relevance to planning, is described in detail and provides an excellent basis for any student wishing to take these issues further.

REFERENCES

Brocklesby, J. and S. Cummings (1996) 'Foucault plays Habermas: an alternative philosophical underpinning for critical systems thinking', *Journal of the Operational Research Society* 47(6): 741–54.

Burrell, G. and G. Morgan (1979) *Sociological Paradigms and Organisational Analysis*, London: Heinemann.

Clarke, S. A. and B. Lehaney (1999) 'Human-centred methods in information systems development: is there a better way forward?', in *Managing Information Technology Resources in Organisations in the Next Millennium* (conference proceedings) Hershey, PA: Idea Group Publishing.

Clarke, S. A. and B. Lehaney (2000) 'Mixing methodologies for information systems development and strategy: a higher education case study', *Journal of the Operational Research Society* 51(5): 542–56.

Eden, C. (1988) 'Cognitive mapping', *European Journal of Operational Research* 36: 1–13.

Eden, C. (1994) 'Cognitive mapping and problem structuring for system dynamics model building', *System Dynamics* 10(2–3): 257–76.

Etzioni, A. (1967) *The Active Society*, New York: Macmillan.

Foong, A. L. F., A. E. Ojuka-Onedo and J. C. Oliga (1997) 'Lifeworld-system, juridification, and critical entrepreneurship', in *Systems for Sustainability: People, Organizations, and Environments* (conference proceedings) Milton Keynes: Plenum.

Habermas, J. (1971) *Knowledge and Human Interests*. Boston, MA: Beacon Press.

Habermas, J. (1976) 'On systematically distorted communication', *Inquiry* **13**: 205–18.

Habermas, J. (1987) *Lifeworld and System: A Critique of Functionalist Reason*, Boston, MA: Beacon Press.

Hirschheim, R., H. K. Klein and M. Newman (1991) 'Information systems development as social action: theoretical perspective and practice', *Omega* **19**(6): 587–608.

Jackson, M. C. (1993) 'Signposts to critical systems thinking and practice: an invited article', *Kybernetes* **22**(5): 11–21.

Kant, I. ([1787] 1929) *Critique of Pure Reason*, London: Macmillan.

Kelly, G. A. (1955) *The Psychology of Personal Constructs*, London: Weidenfeld & Nicolson.

Midgley, G. (1995) 'Mixing methods: developing systemic intervention', Hull University Research Memorandum no. 9.

Oliga, J. C. (1991) 'Methodological foundations of systems methodologies', R. L. Flood and M. C. Jackson (eds), *Critical Systems Thinking: Directed Readings*, Chichester, Sussex: John Wiley, pp. 159–84.

Oliga, J. C. (1996) *Power, Ideology, and Control*, New York: Plenum.

Probert, S. K. (1996) 'Is total systems intervention compelling?', in *Sustainable Peace in the World System, and the Next Evolution of Human Consciousness* (conference proceedings, Budapest, Hungary), Madison, WI: Omni Press.

Ulrich, W. (1983) *Critical Heuristics of Social Planning: A New Approach to Practical Philosophy*, Berne: Haupt.

Ulrich, W. (1988) 'Systems thinking, systems practice, and practical philosophy: a program of research', *Systems Practice* **1**(2): 137–63.

Ulrich, W. (1991) 'Critical heuristics of social systems design', in R. L. Flood and M. C. Jackson (eds), *Critical Systems Thinking: Directed Readings*, Chichester, Sussex: John Wiley, pp. 103–15.

Weber, M. (1947) *The Theory of Social and Economic Organization*, London: The Free Press, Collier Macmillan.

Index